The Real Christmas Story

An Indepth Biblical And
Historical Look Into The
Truths Surrounding The
Birth Of Jesus

Paul R. Pontis

Fairway Press
Lima, Ohio

THE REAL CHRISTMAS STORY

FIRST EDITION
Copyright © 1994 by
Paul R. Pontis

Library of Congress Catalog Card Number: 93-74121

ISBN 1-55673-857-9

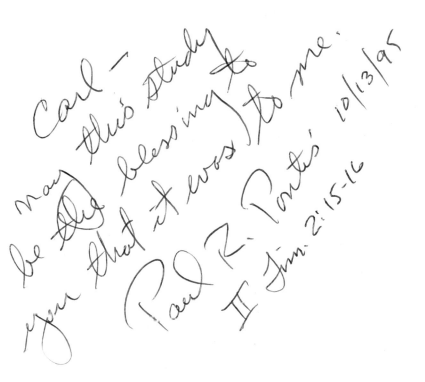

Carl —
May this study be
a blessing to me.
be that it was
Paul R. Pontis
II Tim. 2:15-16
10/13/95

Additional copies of this book may be ordered from
your local Christian bookstore.
$6.95

Quantities may be ordered from:
Paul R. Pontis
536 Cookston Avenue
Springfield, Ohio 45503
513-399-1300

DEDICATION

To the Lord Jesus Christ, the details of Whose birth I have attempted to set forth herein, and to the Holy Spirit, without Whose enlightenment, inspiration and enablement this book would never have been written.

Table of Contents

INTRODUCTION

First Edition

Several years ago I was invited to speak at the annual Christmas banquet of the company from which I am now retired. As I thought on what theme my address might take, this phrase in Matthew 1:18 caught my attention, "Now the birth of Jesus Christ was on this wise."

Probably at that time I was in a more or less state of rebellion against the crass commercialism to which the celebration of Christmas had degenerated. This phrase in Matthew seemed to underscore that contrast between what it was actually like, what really took place when Jesus was born, and what it is actually like when we celebrate His birth today. I had to confess that any similarity was totally lacking.

As I thought further on the matter, I asked myself, "What do you really know about what happened back then and where did you get your information to back up what you think you are sure of?" On both counts I was on rather shaky ground.

Thus it was that I arrived at the theme for the address I was to make at the banquet. More than that, I was launched into a research project on just what the facts were surrounding the birth of Jesus Christ, a research project that spanned almost ten years. In that time I uncovered Bible truth and historical background that has scuttled almost every idea I ever had about the true story of Christmas. The experience has been rewarding, and out of it has come an attempt on my part to record what I learned so I might share it with others.

As I discussed with others the things that I had learned about the facts of Christmas, I soon learned that most of them had the same misconceptions that I had. One person with whom I was discussing the fact that Jesus was not born on December 25th agreed with me immediately, commenting, "That date was set by Congress." I don't know where he got his information, but it has been my experience that what most of us believe about Christmas and the birth of Christ, we have learned either from Christmas cards, favorite stories, or Christmas carols. Only a very small part of what we believe about the events surrounding the birth of Jesus actually came from a study of the Bible.

I was so thrilled over the new truth I had found that I was eager to share it with others. My usual method of sharing is through teaching in a Bible class. But often, I write down an idea or concept to get it properly organized and fixed in my mind before presenting it in class. This I did with these thoughts about the birth of Christ. Each year as Christmas approached I would develop some thoughts further, and as the years passed, the notes accumulated. Occasionally, individuals would ask for copies of these notes, and I would have them typed because my handwriting is not all that good. This was the basis for first one chapter and then another of this book.

When the idea first came to me that these notes might make an interesting book, my original thought was to develop all the facts that I could put together from the Word about each of the primary characters involved in one way or another in the Christmas account. To the fullest extent possible, I wanted to feel that I knew these individuals personally.

As my study continued, many interesting side issues were uncovered that I felt were equally interesting and too important to be left out. *"The fulness of time"* aspect of Galatians 4:4 had to be included if one is going to understand the timing of this fantastically important event in human history. Some background on the customs and culture of the day in which Jesus was born makes the events in the Christmas story really come to life. Other historical considerations make our understanding of these events so much more vivid and beautiful. This is how the text developed.

I have tried to retain my original purpose of emphasizing the individuals involved, but they are seen more in the setting of their history and culture rather than as typical personality studies.

I, personally, am not a theology major, nor did I have unlimited time in which to do original research into the Scriptures. In many instances I have had to draw on the works of others gifted in such research. Though these commentaries and studies were very helpful, I have yet to find this information set down in one continuous account of the events surrounding the birth of Jesus. This is what I have tried to accomplish.

Considering all the hazards in undertaking such a project and in view of the complete improbability that I should ever be considered an author, I take great comfort from that passage in Numbers 22:21-35. In this passage the prophet Balaam is turned from his perverse way because the angel of the Lord was able to make his presence and will known to Balaam's ass, even if Balaam himself could not see. After a while, the ass was caused to speak words of reproach to his master to set him on the path of God's will for Balaam. My comfort comes from the thought that if the angel of the Lord was able to speak through Balaam's ass, surely the Holy Spirit of God could speak through my tongue or my pen, being slightly higher than this dumb servant of old.

Paul tells us in I Corinthians 1:27-29:

"But God hath chosen the foolish things of the world to confound the wise; and God hath chosen the weak things of the world to confound the things which are mighty; And base things of the world, and things which are despised, hath God chosen, yea, and things which are not, to bring to nought things that are: That no flesh should glory in His presence."

Never have I read a more apt description of the author of this book.

If anyone is able to share the blessing that these studies have been to me, then all praise, all glory, and all honor belong to Him who has made all things possible.

Paul R. Pontis

INTRODUCTION

Second Edition

The original limited edition of *The Christmas Story* was published as a booklet by Christian radio station WEEC here in Springfield, Ohio, as a giveaway at Christmas time to those who would write in and request it.

The reception this first limited edition received locally was very gratifying. Many letters of appreciation were received. Some churches used the booklet as a class study guide before the next Christmas, others ordered quantities, and some used the booklet instead of Christmas cards.

When the limited number of copies printed were all gone and requests continued to come in, I decided it was time to consider having the booklet reprinted in a more formal book for wider circulation.

Typical of any first effort, numerous changes in the text were needed to correct punctuation, spelling, grammar and to smooth out the flow of the text. A type that would be easier to read was also needed. Then, additional information that I wanted to include about the "Wise Men" had come to my attention.

With these improvements in mind, this second edition, entitled *Now The Birth Of Jesus Christ Was On This Wise* or *The Real Christmas Story,* is offered with the prayer that it might be a blessing to all who read it, and that it might enable all of us to have a better understanding of the full circumstances surrounding the birth of Jesus our Lord. May this edition bring new dimensions, understanding and spiritual depth to our celebration of Christmas.

Paul R. Pontis

CHAPTER 1

"In the Fulness of Time, Christ Was Born"

Galatians 4:4: "But when the fulness of time was come, God sent forth His son"

In the study of the total Christmas Story, it is necessary for a full understanding of all that God has done for us in the Incarnation, to get a grasp, if we can, of just how full the "fulness of time" was when God sent forth His Son.

From before the foundations of the earth God was working out every detail for the birth of Jesus at this particular time. Even though our Federal head, Adam, had not yet sinned, God the Father and God the Son were planning the details of our salvation, which required that God come to earth in the person of His Son at this *particular* time.

God's foreknowledge of the ultimate sin of Adam and Eve had nothing to do with causing them to sin, but it had everything to do with His planning beforehand for man's salvation once the foreknown sin became a reality.

When, then, should the Son be sent? When should the Christ be born? The answer is summed up in the words of our passage, *"in the fulness of time"* when every detail of the planning and arranging of the Father and Son was complete. It obviously had to be after the sin of Adam, but some 4000 years had elapsed from the creation of man and his sin before Jesus was born. Why all this delay? Why

1

must He wait forty centuries? It was simply because the fulness of time, God's time, had not yet come.

In understanding the timing of God's dealings with man we must always keep in mind that the eternal God knows no time limitations. He lives in one great big NOW. In his second letter, the Apostle Peter explains this fact when he writes,

"But, beloved, be not ignorant of this one thing, that one day is with the Lord as a thousand years, and a thousand years as one day" (II Peter 3:8).

Thus, this 4000 years, which is a very long time to time-bound man, is only as four days with the Lord. It is not even a good week's work.

After the account of the fall of Adam and Eve in Gen. 3 and their expulsion from the Garden, fallen man began to populate the earth spreading his evil nature everywhere he went until God, in judgment, had to wipe out in the Flood, all humanity except Noah, his wife, his three sons and their three wives (Gen. 6:8-7:24), who alone were seen to be righteous; that is, they were living according to God's laws for man at that time.

"And the LORD said unto Noah, Come thou and all thy house into the ark; for thee have I seen righteous before me in this generation" (Gen. 7:1).

But they all still had the fallen nature of Adam, the Federal head of the human race.

Thus, it is no surprise that the descendants of these eight individuals would in time demonstrate the same wickedness and rebellion against God that existed before the flood, which in deed they did. This rebellion against God and His laws manifested itself finally at the Tower of Babel (Gen. 10:32-11:9). Mankind, the descendants of Noah, had rejected God and his plan for them by deciding they were going to get to heaven by their own method and ingenuity. Thus, God confused their languages so that they could no longer communicate and work together. He scattered them into language groups over the earth and rejected mankind of that day as the people through whom He would work to reconcile mankind back to Himself.

Then, we learn in Gen. 11:27-12:3 that God in His sovereignty determined that He would choose one man and his wife, out of all of this scattered, fallen humanity, and through him, create a nation of people, set apart unto Himself for His use in all His dealings with mankind.

Thus, He chose a moon worshipper named Abram who lived in the pagan city of Ur of the Chaldees.

"And Joshua said unto all the people, Thus saith the LORD God of Israel, Your fathers dwelt on the other side of the flood in old time, even Terah, the father of Abraham, and the father of Nachor: and they served other gods" (Josh. 24:2).

From this unlikely prospect God created the nation in which He would center all His dealings with man, the nation that was to be the repository of His written Word to man and His witness to all mankind. It was also to be the nation through which God would send forth His Son to be the Saviour and Redeemer of all mankind, of all times, everywhere.

God is seldom, if ever, in a hurry. So, after about 2000 years of human history had passed, He was content to take this one man and his wife, Sarah, make them wait until Abraham (name changed now from Abram) was 100 years old and his wife was 90, before He gave them their one child of "promise." Yet, with this slow but miraculous start, God created a nation as innumerable as the stars in the heavens for multitudes.

It was one thing for God to create a nation, but quite another to prepare it for His own use. From the days of Abraham, this nation was to be pure, separated from the world about them and set apart for God's own use. Such being the case, even up to the end of their seventy years' captivity by Nebuchadnezzar, king of Babylon, the first of the great Gentile world empires, the nation Israel had a very limited acquaintance with the rest of the world. This acquaintance extended, namely, to the Chaldeans, the Phoenicians, and the Egyptians. Their thoughts and ideas were all centered within their own nation and extended little beyond the teachings of Moses, which were given 1500 years before the end of this captivity.

Still, 500 years stand between Israel's return from captivity and Jesus' birth. Yet when Jesus was crucified, the accusations against Him were written above Him in three different languages: Greek, Latin, and Hebrew.

"And a superscription also was written over him in letters of Greek, and Latin, and Hebrew, This is the King of the Jews" (Luke 23:38).

Where did these first two dialects come from? When the prophets of Israel ended their writings nearly 500 years before this event, the Greek was scarcely a written language and used only in a small portion of Europe. Rome, from which the Latin came, was only a small scattered village on the banks of the Tiber River.

During this 500-year period in which nations and monarchies were born, flourished, and then decayed, showing clearly a providential planning and preparation, there was an intermingling of the various languages that indicates a specific preparation for some great event.

"This matter is by the decree of the watchers, and the demand by the word of the holy ones: to the intent that the living may know that the most High ruleth in the kingdom of men, and giveth it

to whomsoever he will, and setteth up over it the basest of men" (Daniel 4:17).

Surely this was all designed by God to be the most opportune time (the fulness of time) for the introduction of that universal and effective propagation of the gospel. This was that one true religion embodying the knowledge and worship of the one true God through the revelation of Himself in the Person of His Son, Jesus Christ.

Again, going back to the beginning of man, whatever knowledge our earliest ancestors had of God, by the time of Abraham it was completely lost. The nations had generally fallen into idolatry, but God was pleased to make Himself known to Abraham. He promised that of him He would make a great nation. In him and his seed all the nations of the earth would be blessed. This blessing was that through him and his descendants there would be revealed the greatest possible good that could ever come to man, namely, the personal and intimate knowledge of the one true God. And further, to accomplish this purpose, God selected the spot where Abraham and his posterity were to be placed. This was the one spot on earth that was supremely suited to this purpose. This tract of country, originally called Canaan, later Judea, and now Palestine, is situated in the middle of what was then three great divisions of the earth: Asia, Africa, and Europe. It was located on the main highways of conquest, commerce, and travel, and it was equally accessible to all parts of the then known world.

But at the time of Abraham, those circumstances that made Judea the ideal central radiating point for the propagation of this one true faith did not exist, because there was neither conquest, commerce, nor travel. The known world was overrun with wandering tribes that had no boundaries or fixed habitation. Chaldea, the cradle of the human race, and Egypt, the birthplace of human learning and the arts, were the only nations of

5

consequence in Abraham's day. It is doubtful that there was even a written language at this time. Divine communications traveled by word of mouth only. The *"fulness of time"* had not yet come in Abraham's day, to make known even that partial revelation of the one true God revealed later by Moses .

There was no method whereby it could be recorded or preserved. The invention of writing, which took place somewhere in the 500 years that elapsed between Abraham and Moses, was necessary to prepare the world for even this partial revelation.

Thus, to continue the preparation of the family of Israel for His use, God sent them down into Egypt as if He were sending them off to school. In Egypt they not only learned some great spiritual truths by experience, but were also trained in the arts and in the knowledge of those things by which life is made more comfortable. Then, in a circumstance of deep trial and suffering, where all of these comforts were removed, they grew into a nation of suitable size and strength to occupy the territory God had ordained for them. So it was that He then raised up Moses, the child of a slave, to lead His trained people back to their appointed homeland.

It was on this forty-year-long trip home that God gave the Ten Commandments, by using the engraving of letters on stone for the first time.

Back in their own God-given land, with the Law of Moses as their national charter and code of life, they prospered and were strong when they obeyed this Law. But they suffered and were overrun by their enemies when they succumbed to their natural bent to worship idols. In time the temple of Solomon was built. Even this and the Ark of the Covenant could not keep them from reverting to idol worship.

Finally, God's hand of judgment came upon them, and they were carried away into a seventy-year period of captivity. So severe and effective was this punishment that never, after their release from this captivity, did they ever again revert to idol worship. So it was that God, who had turned them into captivity because of their sin of idolatry, released them when they had well learned their lesson. With this release, God told Daniel, the prophet of the times of the Gentiles, that it would be 483 years from the going forth to rebuild the temple to the coming of Messiah.

"Seventy weeks are determined upon thy people and upon thy holy city, to finish the transgression, and to make an end of sins, and to make reconciliation for iniquity, and to bring in everlasting righteousness, and to seal up the vision and prophecy, and to anoint the most Holy.

"Know therefore and understand, that from the going forth of the commandment to restore and to build Jerusalem unto the Messiah the Prince shall be seven weeks, and threescore and two weeks: the street shall be built again, and the wall, even in troublous times.

"And after threescore and two weeks shall Messiah be cut off, but not for himself: and the people of the prince that shall come shall destroy the city and the sanctuary; and the end thereof shall be with a flood, and unto the end of the war desolations are determined.

"And he shall confirm the covenant with many for one week: and in the midst of the week he shall cause the sacrifice and the oblation to cease, and for the overspreading of abominations he shall make it desolate, even until the consummation,

7

and that determined shall be poured upon the desolate" (Daniel 9:24 - 27).

The temple was rebuilt, and the daily worship and sacrifices were restored, and this was not interrupted, except for about three years under Antiochus Epiphanes.

But even at this late date all the nations of the earth, except the Jews, knew nothing of the one true God. Thus, it fell upon the Jews to extend this knowledge to all the world. But because of barrenness and bigotry they were almost rendered useless so far as their being of any help to the rest of the world. God had to intervene again in the affairs of man in general and the Jews in particular so that His ultimate intention for them, as promised to Abraham, could be carried out. All of this was brought about, first, by the universal diffusion of the Greek language, and second, by the conquest of the world by the Romans.

No one but a few of the Jews now knew the Hebrew language for the majority spoke Chaldee, the language of their captors. If there was to be a universal distribution of the knowledge of the one true God, there had to be a universal language. If this truth was to be distributed worldwide, the Jews (who alone knew the truth about this one true God) would have to learn the universal language and then would have to be scattered throughout the world. Seeing the way in which God carried this out will give us some insight into just what Paul meant by "the fulness of time."

Israel and Judah had been taken captive by Nebuchadnezzar some 500 years before Christ was born. In time, Nebuchadnezzar died, and Belshazzar took over the reign of Babylon. He was ultimately captured by Cyrus the Persian in his fantastic and cunning siege of the city to begin the second great Gentile world empire. Cyrus was then succeeded by Darius the Mede, who became King of Persia. It was under his reign that the colonies the Greeks planted in Asia began to rebel against the tribute they were required to pay to Darius. Many bitter skirmishes were fought between these two nations, and in time, the colonies applied to the mother country, Greece, and with the help from Athens and Sparta, they were able to take Sardis, accidentally setting it on fire, burning it to the ground. The loss of this, the richest city in Asia Minor so enraged Darius that he resolved to seek revenge. Before he had his campaign fully organized, he died and Xerxes, his son, began to reign. Xerxes (Ahasuerus) was the king to whom Esther was married. He was four years preparing to fulfill the revenge he inherited from his father. Every province under his rule was required to furnish its quota of ships, troops, or provisions, all this effort to crush this one small, insignificant country (called Greece) on the Adriatic Sea.

Now Greece, in the divine providence of God, had already begun to show her great genius in arts, letters, and science. She had originated political freedom in government, and a few generations of this political liberty had trained a race of men never seen before. Yet, before her stood one of the most formidable forces ever put together by man, under Xerxes. Was all of this progress and culture of Greece to be lost to this despotic Oriental king? Man may have put this great army together, but God was leading it and the Greeks, and Xerxes did not prevail. Instead, he and his armies were sent home as a beaten dog with its tail between its legs, and they never ventured out upon Greece again. This defeat was eventually to show Greece that they were ultimately to be masters of the world.

Greece was a confederated state and combined well for the defense of their nation. They were not sufficiently organized, though, to mount an offensive. Thus, they did not pursue Xerxes, and for 120 years more Persia continued as the second great Gentile world power. During this time, after the Persian invasion, Greece developed more and more as a wonderful nation until her

9

intellectual treasure house was full. More great minds were developed within that country in those years than in any other nation in recorded history up to the time of Christ.

Then, when Greece was under his subjection, Philip, king of Macedonia, began to make plans for conquest in the East. Before he was able to begin his first campaign though, he was assassinated, leaving his kingdom to his son, Alexander, a youth of twenty years. This was 350 years before Christ was born.

It is said that Alexander by his personal endowments and statesmanship did more in twelve years to affect the future of the world than any other uninspired man that ever lived. He was a perfect representative of all that Greece stood for in the way of genius and learning with their valor and conduct. Wherever he went, Greece went with him, for he not only set up monarchies but centers of Grecian learning.

In twelve years he took over the whole Persian Empire, along with many other nations that had never before been subjected to the Persian yoke. He carried the Grecian manners, arts, science, and language to nearly the entire human race in existence. Of course, Judea and the Jews were included, and so it was that under the third great Gentile world empire the Jews were forced to learn Koiné Greek, the most perfect language ever developed and the language of the known world of that day.

Egypt surrendered to Alexander without a single fight. With the instinct of the genius he was, he picked the site for the city on the banks of the west branch of the Nile that was to bear his name. It sprang up immediately and was one of the most beautiful and magnificent cities of the world. Here in Alexandria a large colony was formed where only the Greek language was used. To populate this city the Jews were invited by the most liberal offer. Thus, it became necessary to have the Hebrew scriptures translated into Greek, or the Jews would have lost their knowledge of these scriptures altogether. So it was that seventy scholars produced the Greek text known as the Septuagint Translation that is still a standard of the world today. By this translation was the knowledge of the one true God made known to the entire world. Surely divine providence operates the nations of the earth as a great machine carrying out God's plan.

At about 720 B.C. a small band of Trojan refugees established themselves on the banks of the Tiber River. They were at first a monarchy that lasted for about 200 years. Then they turned to a popular form of government. They were always warlike from the first, but it was not until the establishment of this people's government that their nationalistic character began to rapidly develop, showing strong love of conquest and military glory. Since this character was truly national in scope, no one could hope to succeed in Rome without yielding his every talent to those objectives every citizen had most at heart: the honor of the Roman name and the extension of its dominion over foreign nations.

The country was led by a Senate made up of the most distinguished and influential citizens, and those who had arrived there through the regular grades of the magistracy. It constituted a body that for more than 1000 years was unrivaled in history for talent and for weight of wisdom and experience.

Every Roman, from youth to full age, lived in the eye of his country. No man could be a candidate for any office until he had served his country in camp for ten years. The whole nation was a sort of military school. The Roman army was the most terrible object that ever trod the earth. It was a vast human machine, designed for the subjugation of the world. After the age of seventeen every Roman was liable for the military and could be sent to war at any time. When he arrived at camp, he entered upon

11

a course of life in which ease and luxury were altogether unknown. He began a discipline of hardship that was almost incredible and of which there was no end. Even with this kind of training, it took them 500 years to conquer Italy, and in 200 years more they were rulers of the entire world.

Thus, it was under this fourth great Gentile world empire that two things were accomplished. First, the world was shown what real dedication and training for a cause really were. Paul instructed Timothy to

> *"...endure hardness as a good soldier of Jesus Christ" (II Timothy 2:3).*

Timothy knew exactly what Paul meant because he had the example of the Roman soldier ever before him. If a secular government could command such dedication and hardship in training, what could the Ruler of all the universe expect? It was this kind of discipline and dedication that accomplished the spread of the gospel in the Apostolic days of the church, until Paul could write to the church at Rome,

> *"Your faith is spoken of throughout the whole world" (Romans 1:8).*

Second, it was under this Roman government that the Jews and Christians were scattered throughout the known world. They went everywhere preaching the gospel of Jesus Christ, that all the world might know personally the one true God through Jesus Christ,

> *"...in Whom is all the fulness of the Godhead bodily" (Colossians 2:9).*

At this time and for several hundred years after the end of the Grecian reign, all the world spoke one perfect language. All mankind could hear the message God gave to Abraham 2000 years before, that in Abraham's Seed

12

should all the world be blessed. The Romans had built roads for the missionaries to travel on. All the world was one great nation making the crossing of borders no big thing. Surely then, this was the *"fulness of time when God sent forth His Son."* At no other time in the history of all mankind, before or since the birth of Christ, could it be said that there was a better time for Christ to have been born or that it was a *"fuller time."*

Lest the fact be overlooked, the birth of Jesus in Bethlehem of Judea was exactly 483 years from the issuing of the decree by Cyrus, King of Persia that the temple at Jerusalem should be rebuilt, even as Daniel was shown by the angel Gabriel.

> *"Now in the first year of Cyrus king of Persia, that the word of the Lord spoken by the mouth of Jeremiah might be accomplished, the Lord stirred up the spirit of Cyrus king of Persia, that he made a proclamation throughout all his kingdom, and put it also in writing, saying,*
>
> *"Thus saith Cyrus king of Persia, All the kingdoms of the earth hath the Lord God of heaven given me; and he hath charged me to build him an house in Jerusalem, which is in Judah. Who is there among you of all his people? The Lord his God be with him, and let him go up"* (II Chronicles 36:22,23).

To me it is quite interesting that the very first verses of the next book in the Bible repeats this command of Cyrus almost word for word.

> *"Now in the first year of Cyrus king of Persia, that the word of the Lord by the mouth of Jeremiah might be fulfilled, the Lord stirred up the spirit of Cyrus king of Persia, that he made a proclamation throughout all his kingdom, and put it also in writing, saying,*

13

"Thus saith Cyrus king of Persia, The Lord God of heaven hath given me all the kingdoms of the earth; and he hath charged me to build him an house at Jerusalem, which is in Judah.

"Who is there among you of all his people? his God be with him, and let him go up to Jerusalem, which is in Judah, and build the house of the Lord God of Israel, (he is the God), which is in Jerusalem.

"And whosoever remaineth in any place where he sojourneth, let the men of his place help him with silver, and with gold, and with goods, and with beasts, beside the freewill offering for the house of God that is in Jerusalem" (Ezra 1:1 - 4).

"The fulness of time" had come, and all things were indeed ready for the birth of the Messiah of Israel, the Saviour of all mankind, indicating the foreknowledge and timing of God. Truly, this was the pre-eminent hour of history.

This hour, the coming of the Lord Jesus, is expressed in the New Testament as occurring at a particularly divinely appointed time. At the beginning of Mark (1:15) we read, *"The TIME is fulfilled"* Then again in our passage in Galatians 4:4, Paul writes,

"But when the fulness of the TIME was come, God sent forth his Son, made of a woman, made under the law."

And the Apostle Peter in his first epistle referred to Christ as;

"manifest in these last TIMES for you" (I Peter 1:20).

Also, we have these two Scriptures that are related to the death of Christ as well as to His birth:

14

"in due TIME Christ died for the ungodly" (Romans 5:6).

"but now once in the end of the world (at the conjunction of the ages) hath He [Christ] appeared to put away sin by the sacrifice of himself" (Hebrews 9:26).

Now we might well ask ourselves this question, "In what way was the Advent and Crucifixion of our Lord, in the early part of the first century (from 5 B.C. to 30 A.D.) the 'end of the world [age]'"?

First, as we have already pointed out, the whole known world was then one vast empire such as it had never been before and would never be again. There were 3000 miles of Roman Empire from the Euphrates River to the Atlantic Ocean with 120 million souls, over half of which were slaves.

Peace, of a type, ruled throughout the world for this one remarkable brief period; thus men were not occupied with the exhausting distractions and destructions of war but were free to listen to the gospel message of the Lord Jesus.

As there was one world government, so there was one generally used language, the Greek in which our New Testament was written, one language with which man could preach from Babylon to Spain. It would not be long before this union of states would break up into national tongues.

Not only externally, but also internally, the end of the age was manifest. Men lost faith in God and spurned their goddesses. They attempted to substitute the deification of the Roman Empire or to become devotees of Oriental cults of superstition and magic.

Cicero, in the Roman Forum, could laugh at the gods of Rome. This would never have happened a century before. The sense of certitude was gone, and skepticism reigned everywhere. Philosophy was developing stoicism or a pagan pantheism. Among the educated class, materialism was everywhere present. This bankruptcy of philosophy and religion was accompanied by cruelty and lust everywhere. In one month, 20,000 gladiators hacked each other to pieces to satisfy the Romans' lust for blood. The great historian Tacitus wrote, "To corrupt and be corrupt, was the spirit of the time."

The Roman Empire was moving toward an abyss of despair and destruction when, at the *"end of the age,"* where much later it would be too late,

"God sent forth His Son, made of a woman, made under the law" (Galatians 4:4).

Never were there so many magicians, incantations, or so many false cults. It was indeed *"the end of the age," "the fulness of time."*

The epoch of religious experience had passed into an epoch of despair, and it was now time for a message of hope.

Every timepiece of God had run out, and a fantastic chorus of chimes from all over the universe hailed that *"the fulness of time"* had indeed come. Thus it was at this pre-eminent time in the history of mankind that Jesus, the Christ, was born!

CHAPTER 2

"Made of a Woman, Made under the Law"
(Galatians 4:4)

Apart from the Christ Child Himself, the central person in the total account of the birth of Christ is Mary, His mother. It is in Mary's experience with the Holy Spirit that the main body of the Christmas story is introduced.

We do not know everything we might like to know about Mary. Scripture gives us only the lineage of her family. It tells us little about her family life. Most of this has to be gleaned from historical accounts.

If the betrothal of Mary and Joseph was typical of their time, Joseph would not think of marriage until he was at least twenty-five years of age. However, it was quite customary for girls to marry soon after puberty. Mary could well have been in her middle teens at the time of her betrothal to Joseph. Such early marriages were often a matter of economics in the typically poor communities such as Nazareth of Galilee.

Though the marriages were arranged between the parents of the couple, it did not necessarily indicate that the couple had no say in the marriage, nor that it was totally lacking in love. On the contrary, in a small hamlet like Nazareth, with just one well for water (still existing today), everyone in the town knew each other. Joseph and Mary would very likely have met and visited, either at the well or at one of the annual festivals, the usual source of recreation and celebration.

As Joseph began to contemplate marriage, he would have asked his parents if he could marry that village girl, a distant relative, Mary, the daughter of Heli (compare Judges 14:1-10). The parents would have then discussed the request between themselves before giving their answer. They would have carefully appraised Mary's parental background, her ancestry, resources, temperament, and reputation. Of all these qualifications, the resources would have been of least importance because everyone in Nazareth was poor.

They could hardly have found fault with Mary's ancestry because it was the same as their own. Although both families were of quite modest circumstances, both were also direct descendants of the royal family of Israel. Each family could proudly trace its family tree back to King David. Considering this, it would have been no problem for Joseph's parents to approve his choice with much enthusiasm. (See Joseph's family tree in Matthew 1:1-8 and Mary's family tree in Luke 3:23-38.)

Joseph's father, Jacob, would have visited Mary's parents, who would have acted duly surprised at the purpose of the visit. Nevertheless, Mary's offhand comments in the past to her parents about the young carpenter, Joseph, the son of Jacob, could already have established her interest. Discussions could have begun in earnest with the two fathers doing most of the negotiating. In Biblical times, marriage was considered a covenant between the two families, not just between the participants. There were many matters to be discussed in addition to the dowry, which would have been small, at best.

Finally, the happy fathers would have agreed to a marriage contract between their children, but as has been shown, the bride and groom would not have been simply thrown at each other in a loveless match. The direct or indirect comments of the boy and girl would have indicated the timing and which family to contact. Love was indeed a factor in such marriages, and because mature adults discussed the merits and demerits of such alliances, many of the pitfalls common to our modern-day engagements were avoided.

Once the marriage contract was formalized, Joseph was then undoubtedly brought before Mary while both of their parents spoke a formal benediction over them as the couple sipped a cup of wine. This, the legal betrothal, was far more binding than the modern engagement of today. Only a divorce could break it. The usual period of betrothal was one year, but this waiting period could have been shortened by the marriage contract. At the end of the betrothal the marriage ceremony was celebrated, and from that time on the couple lived as man and wife.

If during this waiting period either Joseph or Mary had been proven unfaithful, even though they were not yet married, this unfaithfulness would have been considered an adultery, punishable by death. Also, if Joseph had died during this betrothal period, Mary would have been his legal widow. Specific regulations for an unfaithful woman who might be betrothed, as Mary was to Joseph, are given in Deuteronomy 22:23-24:

> *"If a damsel that is a virgin be betrothed unto an husband, and a man find her in the city, and lie with her;*
>
> *"Then ye shall bring them both out unto the gate of that city, and ye shall stone them with stones that they die; the damsel, because she cried not, being in the city; and the man because he hath humbled his neighbour's wife: so thou shalt put away evil from among you."*

19

One of the purposes of this year of waiting was to make sure that the groom was marrying a chaste virgin. This virtue was prized above all others and was guarded most carefully by the girl's parents. In Deuteronomy 22:13-19 we read,

> *"If any man take a wife, and go in unto her, and hate her,*
>
> *"And give occasions of speech against her, and bring up an evil name upon her, and say, I took this woman, and when I came to her, I found her not a maid:*
>
> *"Then shall the father of the damsel, and her mother, take and bring forth the tokens of the damsel's virginity unto the elders of the city in the gate:*
>
> *"And the damsel's father shall say unto the elders, I gave my daughter unto this man to wife, and he hateth her;*
>
> *"And, lo, he hath given occasions of speech against her, saying, I found not thy daughter a maid; and yet these are the tokens of my daughter's virginity. And they shall spread the cloth before the elders of the city.*
>
> *"And the elders of that city shall take that man and chastise him;*
>
> *"And they shall amerce him in (fine him) an hundred shekels of silver, and give them unto the father of the damsel, because he hath brought up an evil name upon a virgin of Israel: and she shall be his wife; he may not put her away all his days."*

This portion of Scripture describes what we would consider some rather strange customs that depict to what lengths the parents of a young maiden would go to prove that their daughter was, indeed, the chaste virgin they knew her to be. If it was found that the bride was not the virgin she was presented to be, or if she had been proven unfaithful, the groom could simply write her a legal bill of divorcement and send her quietly on her way. However, if he was of such a mind, he could make a public spectacle of her, put her to open, public shame, and ultimately have her put to death by stoning. Such action was what the scribes and Pharisees had in mind in John 8:1-11 concerning the woman taken in adultery. They came to Jesus in the temple, stones in hand. Promiscuity was a very serious crime in the Jewish economy under which Mary and Joseph lived.

It was in this period of waiting that we pick up the accounts of the birth of Christ in both Matthew 1:18-25 and in Luke 1:26-56. It is in Matthew's account that we learn of God's dealing with Joseph in relation to this miraculous birth. Also, Matthew tells us of the coming of the "Magi." It is from Luke's account that we get our best insight into Mary, the person, and the Holy Spirit's working with her as well as His watchful care over her.

The political situation in Israel is dealt with later in this story, but it would help to have a look at "spiritual Israel" in order to better appreciate the setting of Mary's experience.

In Mary's day, as in the days of Samuel in the Old Testament, there was little or no open revelation of God to Israel.

> *"And the child Samuel ministered unto the Lord before Eli. And the word of the Lord was precious in those days; there was no open vision" (I Sam. 3:1).*

Except for a few isolated islands of faith and fidelity such as Mary herself, Zacharias the priest, and ancient

21

Simeon and Anna, most of the spiritual leaders of Israel were thoroughly corrupt. This fact is born out by secular history, by Luke's account, and by the later teachings of Christ. Unbelief was rampant.

In this setting we read;

"And in the sixth month the angel Gabriel was sent from God unto a city of Galilee, named Nazareth,

"To a virgin espoused [engaged] to a man whose name was Joseph, of the house of David; and the virgin's name was Mary [meaning approximately 'The Lord's beloved']" (Luke 1:26-27).

Twice in Luke 1:27, Mary is said to be a virgin, undoubtedly to emphasize the nature and character of this one who was chosen of God for the work He wants to do. This is in complete fulfillment of the prophecy of Isaiah 7:14 where Israel is promised a miraculous sign from the Lord.

"Therefore the Lord himself shall give you a sign; Behold, a virgin shall conceive, and bear a son, and shall call his name Immanuel [God with us]."

The account continues in Luke 1:28:

"And the angel came in unto her, and said, HAIL, THOU THAT ART HIGHLY FAVOURED, THE LORD IS WITH THEE: BLESSED ART THOU AMONG WOMEN."

We have read or heard this account so many times that the angel's greeting is almost commonplace to us, we know it by heart. But just for a moment, let us try to relive this experience as it happened to Mary. We are not told where Mary was or what she was doing at the time the angel Gabriel came to her. The Archko Volume (page 82) tells of an interview between Mary and one Gamaliel wherein Mary said that the angel appeared to her "one day when she was grinding some meal." From all appearances there was no build-up to this. In an instant, the same angel, Gabriel, who had appeared to Zacharias the priest, now appeared to Mary, proclaiming;

"HAIL, THOU THAT ART HIGHLY FAVOURED, THE LORD IS WITH THEE: BLESSED ART THOU AMONG WOMEN."

Keep in mind that there was no precedent for this in Mary's day. The same experience when it occurred in the temple to the aged and faithful priest, Zacharias, literally struck fear into his heart. If such an experience could so trouble one who had ministered before the Lord so faithfully and blamelessly for years, what would a similar experience do to a teen-age girl? How does an angel appear and disappear? What does he look like, and how does an angel sound when he delivers such a greeting as:

"Hail, thou that art highly favoured, the Lord is with thee: blessed art thou among women."

Surely Zacharias should have expected to meet God every time he went into the temple because God had told Israel that this was the place where He would meet them. But for God to speak, even through His messenger Gabriel, to a teen-age girl was unheard of and startling to say the least. (Compare Judges 6:11-13.)

Luke 1:29 tells us Mary's reaction:

"And when she saw him, she was troubled at his saying, and cast in her mind what manner of salutation this should be."

Mary's reaction was typical of most teen-agers: "WHO? ME!?" Yes, Mary you. "BUT WHY ME?" These thoughts and expressions of Mary's, mixed with the

23

surprise and fear that most surely gripped her heart at that initial greeting showed through her countenance. Thus the angel's first act in Mary's behalf, as it was with Zacharias, was to remove all fear.

> *"And the angel said unto her 'Fear not, Mary'"*
> *(Luke 1:30).*

I John 4:18 tells us that, *"perfect love casteth out fear."*

And God's *"perfect love"* for all mankind, including Mary, was about to burst forth in all of its fantastic glory. Surely, the word of the day both to Zacharias (Luke 1:13), to Mary (Luke 1:30), to the shepherds (Luke 2:10), to Joseph (Matthew 1:20), and to all the Lord's followers of all ages (Matthew 10:28 & 31; Luke 5:10, 8:50, 12:32; John 12:15; Acts 27:24; II Timothy 1:7) was *"FEAR NOT,"* for the Savior of the whole world is come.

Then, the angel goes on to tell Mary why she had been chosen. Simply;

> *"Fear not, Mary: for thou hast found favor with*
> *God" (Luke 1:30).*

The Amplified New Testament translates Luke 1:30 this way,

> *"Do not be afraid, Mary, for you have found grace*
> *- - free, spontaneous, absolute favor, and loving*
> *kindness - - with God."*

So, why had Mary been chosen? For the same reason any servant of God, in any age, is chosen, on the basis of the grace of God alone. On the basis of the unmerited loving kindness of God, and in no merit of ourselves whatsoever.

This messenger went on to explain to Mary that God wanted to do a great, miraculous, and marvelous work in her, and He needed her body as one of His tools in bringing this miraculous work to pass as Luke 1:31 implies;

"And, behold, thou shalt conceive in thy womb, and bring forth a Son, and thou shalt call his name JESUS" (Luke 1:31).

The angel was simply asking Mary's permission to use her body in this way. And his arguments in favor of her obedience are to show Mary the glorious outcome of her agreeing to be so used. At no time does he mention anything of the problems, heartaches, or possible consequences that such agreement might bring. All of these Mary would have to trust to the faithfulness of the One who had called her to this work.

So the angel Gabriel continues his explanation to Mary, of the total meaning of this visitation, as he says,

"And, behold, thou shalt conceive in thy womb, and bring forth a Son, and thou shalt call his name JESUS" (Luke 1:31).

And all the while Mary is casting about in her mind wondering

"How shall this be, seeing I know not a man?" (Luke 1:34)

and I'm already given to Joseph. *"How can these things be?"*

But the angel continues his message from God, saying,

"He shall be great, and shall be called the Son of the Highest, and the Lord God shall give unto Him the throne of His father David" (Luke 1:32).

What daughter of David didn't secretly thrill at the possibility that she might be the one, chosen of God, to fulfill this prophecy? It was promised to David, that

25

through his family, the Saviour of Israel and all mankind should come. Not just any son, but THE SON, "JESUS" which means literally, "Jehovah is salvation." So His Name was called. But the thought persisted in Mary's mind,

> *"How shall this be, seeing I know not a man?"*
> *(Luke 1:34)*

And the angel continues,

> *"And He shall reign over the house of Jacob for ever; and of His kingdom there shall be no end*
> *(Luke 1:33).*

I can imagine Mary's thoughts at this point. How wonderful, how glorious, to think that I, Mary, the daughter of Heli, a poor peasant of this lowly village of Nazareth (compare John 1:46) should be chosen out of all the women of the family of David. Me, in my low estate, to be the Mother of the Saviour of Israel. Yea, the Saviour of all mankind, past, present and future. But, Mary finally asks,

> *"How shall this be, seeing I know not a man?"*
> *(Luke 1:34)*

You see, regardless of how wonderful all the works were that the angel Gabriel described, regardless of what fruit God wanted to produce in Mary's body, it was all utterly impossible so far as any strength or capability Mary may have had, even if she had "known" a man.

So it is that the angel answers this young girl's honest doubts. It must be the work of God in you, Mary, for

> *"The Holy Spirit shall come upon thee, and the power of the Highest shall overshadow thee"*
> *(Luke 1:35).*

The work is all God's work, Mary, and none of your own. The Son of the Highest, Mary, must be the product of the power of the Highest. Man can have no part in it whatsoever.

"Therefore, also that Holy Thing which shall be born of thee shall be called the Son of God" (Luke 1:35).

And listen carefully, Mary, the angel continues,

"thy cousin Elisabeth, she hath also conceived a son in her old age and this is the sixth month with her who is called (had a reputation for being) barren" (Luke 1:36).

In an instant Mary is reminded that it doesn't make any difference whether it involves God making a man from the dust of the earth, a woman from the rib of that man, or using a barren 90 year old Sarah and 100 year old Abraham, who, the Word tells us, were as good as dead (Romans 4:19), or Zacharias and his barren wife, Elisabeth; both of whom were well stricken in years, or even Mary, a young virgin maiden. The implication is this. Don't look on the weakness of the flesh, Mary, but rather, look to God who is doing the work.

"For with God, NOTHING shall be impossible" (Luke 1:37).

Just let God have your body, Mary. Surrender it completely to Him. Sure, there are many things about this conception and birth of which I speak that neither you, nor Joseph, nor your parents, nor all mankind will ever understand. Never-the-less, leave this uncertainty and all the possible consequences to God, and see all the truly great things He will do in and through you. In light of the mercies of God extended to you, Mary, present your body a living sacrifice, holy, as only He can make it holy, acceptable unto Him as only He can make it so. For it is

27

indeed, in the light of His great mercies, your "reasonable service" unto Him. (Compare Rom. 12:1) All of this is implied in the angel's words to Mary.

And so it was that Mary said unto the angel, Gabriel;

"Behold the handmaid of the Lord, be it unto me according to thy word" (Luke 1:38).

Thus, Mary surrendered her body unto God to use as He saw fit, regardless of the outcome. As quickly and quietly as he had come the angel departed. All he asked of Mary was a definite act of her will, for God cannot use any person against his will. Mary expressed her willingness to be used of God, and it was at this point that the Holy Spirit took over.

Few who read Luke 1:38 have any idea of all that Mary surrendered when she made that specific and pointed commitment of her body and will to the Spirit of God. What did she mean when she referred to herself as, *"the handmaid of the Lord?"* This term *"handmaid"* actually refers to *"a female bond slave."* Now bond slaves in Mary's day had only one thing going for them, they were human beings. Beyond that they had nothing. They owned no property, they were property themselves. They had absolutely no rights. Their masters could do with them as they pleased. There were no laws governing their treatment, and they had no rights of appeal. They were used as their masters saw fit wherever he pleased to send them. They were indeed not their own. They were bought, body, soul and spirit with a price, and it was expected that in every conceivable way they would live to please their master. Mary, in the declaration of her commitment unto her Lord, was expressing this very attitude. Her statement could read, *"You are looking at a female bond slave of God. You have my body, soul, and spirit, to use as you have said."* No fuller commitment has ever been made. Yet, the Lord Jesus is referred to as a *"bond slave"* in Philippians 2:5 (the word "servant" should be translated *"bond slave."*). The New Testament characters, Paul, Peter, John, Timothy, Titus and Jude, all refer to themselves, and the Christian believers of all ages in exactly the same way, as bond slaves. Thus, Mary accepted the position of a bond slave in order to give birth to a Bond Slave so that you and I could be the same.

Yes, Mary surrendered herself completely to God, to use as He saw fit. But she was still betrothed to Joseph, and there were still the Levitical Laws governing adultery. Such being the case, try to imagine, if you can, the thoughts that must have raced through Mary's young mind as the angel departed from her. She had never seen an angel before, and, so far as she knew, no one else of her acquaintance had either. Was her experience real, or was it just a dream? Was she really "with child?" How could she have possibly known? There was no physical contact with anyone. Mary still had not *"known a man."* The angel described the manner of her conception when he said unto her,

"The Holy Spirit shall come upon thee, and the power of the Highest shall overshadow thee" **(Luke 1:35).**

Then, as soon as Mary gave consent for her body to be so used of God the angel departed from her. Was she really with child as the angel had said? How could she possibly know? If she was, who would understand?

In the Williams translation of Matthew 1:18 we read,

"Now the birth of Jesus Christ occurred under these conditions: After His mother, Mary, was engaged to Joseph, but before they had lived together (as man and wife) she was found to be an expectant mother through the influence of the Holy Spirit."

29

Now, Mary knew this was true, and God knew it was true, but who else would ever believe such a preposterous claim? In this matter Mary now had absolutely no defense whatsoever. Whether with Joseph himself, or with the parents who had arranged their betrothal, or with other relatives, friends or acquaintances. The reproach of all the Law of Moses relative to infidelity and promiscuity stood before her. Her only recourse now was to God, unto Whom she had surrendered her body. If God did not take care of her, execution by stoning was a very real possibility.

It has been said, that, "Until a person has trusted God for something, wherein, if God does not graciously intercede in his behalf, he is literally "sunk," that person has not *really* trusted God at all." Mary had committed herself to God in just such a way. For her, there was absolutely no turning back. God, and God alone, had to intercede for her, or she was, indeed, literally "sunk." What would you do now if you were Mary? To whom could she possibly turn in this hour of tremendous need?

As Mary thought on this new crisis that was now so very much a vital part of her every waking moment, I am sure that the Spirit of that new Life which was in her, brought to her remembrance the one person in all of Judah who could understand, her cousin Elisabeth. Hadn't the angel told Mary that God had intervened in this aged couple's life, and, in spite of their great age, and Elisabeth's historic barrenness, Elisabeth was now in the sixth month of her expectancy? Surely, if anyone could understand, it would be Elisabeth. Didn't she also know a miraculous conception as the angel had said? And so, Mary concludes, "I must talk to Elisabeth."

Thus, it was, as Luke 1:39 tells us that;

"Mary arose in those days and went into the hill country with haste, into a city of Judah."

To make such a journey Mary would have undoubtedly joined a caravan going that way since it would have been unsafe for a young woman to travel the route alone.

Although the scriptures are not specific on this matter, I believe it is reasonable to assume, in light of the wording here, that Mary went to see Elisabeth without having told her parents or Joseph of this new development in her life. Mary couldn't be sure herself if she was really "with child" at this early date. The expression in Luke 1:39 that *"Mary went into the hill country with haste,"* carries the idea that it was shortly after her visitation with the angel. The Living Bible translates Luke 1:39-40 this way,

"A few days later Mary hurried to the highlands of Judea to the town where Zacharias lived, to visit Elizabeth."

So, if Mary didn't know for sure, what would be the point in telling anyone else? Who would believe her? Only Elisabeth.

So Mary went with haste,

"And entered into the house of Zacharias and saluted Elizabeth," (Luke 1:40).

That is all, Mary just greeted her. In that brief moment of greeting, without Mary even mentioning her visitation by the angel, the spirit of Christ, yet unborn, yea, only having been conceived for a few days, bore witness with the spirit of John, also not yet born. And John, Elisabeth reports,

"leaped for joy" (Luke 1:41)

within her. And also, Elisabeth was, in the moment of that witness, filled with the Holy Spirit. What a fantastic experience that must have been, spirit bearing witness with spirit, and the Holy Spirit literally permeating the total scene. But, on the other hand, isn't this the way Spirit-filled believers should be?

Typical of those who are truly Spirit-filled;

"It came to pass, that, when Elisabeth heard the salutation of Mary, the babe leaped in her womb; and Elisabeth was filled with the Holy Spirit: And she spake out with a loud voice, and said, Blessed art thou among women, and blessed is the fruit of thy womb" (Luke 1:41-42).

Elisabeth witnesses to Mary of the reality of the presence of Christ, the Messiah of Israel, and Elisabeth's Lord, in the womb of Mary. At this moment, Mary now knows for sure that she is indeed with child as the angel had said. What blessed assurance, what peace these words must have spoken to Mary's heart, not only that she was indeed "with child," but also, that God was going before, preparing the way, interceding in wonderful ways in her behalf. How marvelously God is working. Yet, should we be surprised? Should we have expected otherwise? It was not necessary that Mary tell Elisabeth anything, and then wonder if she would believe it. Elisabeth told Mary, from information the Holy Spirit gave her, what Mary needed to hear. And then, Elisabeth continues her witness, and from the wording it is difficult to tell whether she is speaking to Mary, to God in prayer and praise, or to others in her home, for she did speak in a loud voice. And in this witness, we find the key to God's being able to work in such a marvelous and miraculous way in Mary's life. In Luke 1:45, Elisabeth says;

"And blessed is she that believed: for there shall be a performance of those things which were told her from the Lord."

"Blessed is she that BELIEVED: for there shall be a PERFORMANCE." The basis of the performance was

Mary's belief, her absolute confidence in God's call to her, and the complete yielding of her body to Him for His use.

The apostle Paul wrote to the believers at Rome,

"I beseech you therefore, brethren, by the mercies of God, that ye present your bodies a living sacrifice, holy, acceptable unto God, which is your reasonable service" (Romans 12:1).

That which God asked of Mary, and she responded to so completely, is exactly what God is asking of us in this passage in Romans. God is in heaven, and thus, He has no need of a body. Indeed, no body could contain Him, for He occupies all eternity. (Isaiah 57:15). Jesus Christ, when He was here on earth, had His own Body which He received from Mary as a result of the surrender of her own body to the use God had in mind for it. Now that Jesus has been taken out of this world, and has sent His Holy Spirit to take His place, and since the Holy Spirit is actually a disembodied Spirit, having no body of His own, He can only dwell among men as we, like Mary, present our bodies unto Him as living sacrifices for the Holy Spirit to use, as He sees fit. And Paul adds:

"This is no more than your reasonable service" (Rom. 12:1).

Mary presented her body to God, in reality, as a living sacrifice for the Holy Spirit to use, so that Jesus might have this miraculous birth into the world. Thus, the Holy Spirit, literally, produced the life of Christ in her body. Then, Christ in turn, presented His physical Body to God, literally, as a living sacrifice on Calvary's cross, so that we, by the same Spirit's power, might experience the miraculous new birth into His Body, the Church, through faith in His finished work on our behalf. Now, we are each asked to present our bodies in the same way; a living sacrifice for the Holy Spirit's use, so that He can reproduce the life of Christ in us. And, through us, bring others into

His Body, through this new birth process. Have you made such a commitment as this? God, alone, knows what the outcome could be. Do it today; right now.

Surely, it can be said of Mary, even as it was said of her Son, Jesus Christ, that she, for the joy that was set before her, endured the cross, her death to self; and despised the shame, that shame that she was soon to face as she went back to Nazareth. What joy was hers. What peace she would know. How full she was of the wonder, glory, and mercy of God, as she spoke from all her fullness in Luke 1:46-55. No priest of old, or prophet of God ever spoke more wondrous and glorious truth than did this teen-age girl on this occasion. Study these verses and let the Spirit speak to you from them, as He did to Mary as she spoke them.

"And Mary said, My soul doth magnify the Lord, And my spirit hath rejoiced in God my Saviour. For he hath regarded the low estate of his handmaiden: for, behold, from henceforth all generations shall call me blessed. For he that is mighty hath done to me great things; and holy is his name. And his mercy is on them that fear him from generation to generation. He hath showed strength with his arm; he hath scattered the proud in the imagination of their hearts. He hath put down the mighty from their seats, and exalted them of low degree. He hath filled the hungry with good things; and the rich he hath sent empty away. He hath holpen his servant Israel, in remembrance of his mercy; As he spake to our fathers, to Abraham, and to his seed for ever" (Luke 1:46-55).

I seem to sense as I read this account from Luke's Gospel that as wondrous and strange as Mary's meeting with the angel Gabriel was, and glorious as the promises were that he gave to her from God, including the conception by the Holy Spirit, the real mountain top experience for Mary took place a few days later in the home of Zacharias and Elisabeth in the hill country of Judea. Here, for three months, Mary and Elisabeth reveled in the wonder of all that the Holy Spirit was doing in their bodies. But typical of all mountain top experiences, it must ultimately come to an end. They had to get down to the business and reality of every day living. Mary was bound to have been strengthened in this experience, and she was now infinitely more prepared for what lay before her than she was right after her encounter with the angel. But, isn't this the purpose of all such mountain top experiences? To prepare us more fully for the work, the difficulties, the testings and the valley experiences that lie ahead? It is wrong to cling to the experience; except as the memory of it is the basis of greater faith and confidence in our going on for the Lord Who provided the experience in the first place.

And so it was with Mary. Three months have gone by now, and Elisabeth's time is up. Thus, Mary must go back to her own home, her family, her friends and to Joseph. What would they think, what would they say? Would they believe Mary's report as Elisabeth had? Would God still be going before her as was the case with her cousin? She would soon find out, for a teen-ager three months with child, is beginning to appear rather obvious.

We are not told how her parents or friends reacted, but it is certain that Joseph, to whom she was engaged, was not inclined to believe her story. We pick up the account now in Matthew 1:18 where we read,

"When as His mother Mary was espoused (actually engaged or betrothed) to Joseph, before they came together (as man and wife) she was found with child of the Holy Spirit."

In this period of waiting, designed to prove the virginity and cleanliness of the bride, Joseph's bride was found to be three months along with child. Now, Mary knows, and the scriptures tell us who the Father of the child is, but all that Joseph knows is that it is not his child.

We are not told of any conversation between Mary and Joseph, where Mary told him the whole account of her experience with the angel, or the visit and experience at her cousin Elisabeth's home. But the wording of Matt. 1:20-23 seems to imply, that some such conversation took place.

"But while he thought on these things, ...

What things? The things that Mary had told him.

... behold, the angel of the Lord appeared unto him in a dream, saying, Joseph, thou son of David, fear not to take unto thee Mary thy wife: for that which is conceived in her is of the Holy Spirit. And she shall bring forth a son, and thou shalt call his name JESUS: for he shall save his people from their sins. Now all this was done, that it might be fulfilled which was spoken of the Lord by the prophet, saying, Behold, a virgin shall be with child, and shall bring forth a son, and they shall call his name Emmanuel, which being interpreted is, God with us" (Matt. 1:20-23).

The angel's wording of his assurance to Joseph conveys also the idea of a confirmation of things Joseph has already heard.

But, before this pronouncement of the angel to Joseph in his dream, all he knew was that Mary, whom he thought of so highly, and held such great value for, was now under suspicion of one of the most despicable of all crimes. Could this really be true of Mary? How could he possibly have been so deceived about the one of whom he thought so much? How could this one from whom he had expected so much, disappoint him so completely? Joseph is reluctant to believe such ill thoughts about the one whom he had esteemed to be such a good woman. Yet the matter, as bad and inexcusable as it is, is also too plain to be denied. Mary was three months along with child, and did anyone ever hear a more preposterous story? She says she is with child of the Holy Spirit. This was simply more than even a *"just man"* could swallow.

And so we read in Matt 1:19,

"Then Joseph her husband, being a just man and not willing to make her a public example (as provided in Deuteronomy 22:23-24)* *was* **minded to put her away privately."**

That is, his present attitude of mind was to give a bill of divorcement into her hands in the presence of two witnesses, and so, hush the matter as quickly and quietly as possible and send her on her way. *"Being a just man,"* that is, a strict observer of the Law of Moses, Joseph would not go ahead with the marriage for fear of bringing upon his own good name some measure of guilt or reproach. But, also, being a devout man, his devotion to God manifested itself in mercy, And who knows, could her story actually be true? Could this child she is carrying be the SON OF GOD?

But Mary had committed herself fully and completely to God for His will and way to be accomplished in her. She had already found Him to be absolutely trustworthy, and capable of caring for her in this new experience in her

---

* If a damsel *that is* a virgin be betrothed unto an husband, and a man find her in the city, and lie with her; Then ye shall bring them both out unto the gate of that city, and ye shall stone them with stones that they die; the damsel, because she cried not, *being* in the city; and the man, because he hath humbled his neighbour's wife: so thou shalt put away evil from among you. Deuteronomy 22:23-24.

life, yea, this new experience, unique to all mankind. Joseph's attitude could well have been cause for great heartache to Mary. She knew the Divine origin of her conception, but how could she possibly prove it?

In God's selection of Mary for this specific work, never had any daughter of Eve been so dignified, exalted and blessed. Yet, at the same time she was in danger of falling under the condemnation of one of the worst crimes of her day. She could very well be dealt with as a harlot. Some commentators have reported, but without any foundation, that she and Joseph were both subjected to the water test of Numbers 5:12-31 but passed the ordeal successfully. Yet, we do not find that Mary tormented herself about all these horrible possibilities, but rather, being fully aware of her own innocence, kept her mind calm, and committed her cause to Him that judgeth all things righteously. And, again, in the case of Joseph, Mary's faith in the Shepherd of her soul was completely vindicated, for we read in Matt. 1:20,

"But while he thought on these things, behold, the angel of the Lord appeared unto him in a dream, saying 'Joseph thou son of David, fear not to take unto thee, Mary, thy wife: for that which is conceived in her is of the Holy Spirit.'"

God was now beginning to work in Joseph's life, even as He did in Mary's, and in her cousin Elisabeth's life.

"But while he thought on these things..." In this phrase we begin to get a little better insight into the man Joseph. Not only was he a "just man," meaning a strict observer of the Law of Moses and the teachings of God, but he was a level headed man who attempted to think things through, before acting. He was not one to "act in haste and repent in leisure." This was a very serious matter he was confronted with, and it involved one he apparently cared for very much. Thus, he obviously thought much

about his ultimate decision; for it is the "thoughtful," not the "unthinking," whom God is pleased to guide. And as Joseph meditated, apparently he dropped off to sleep. As he slept, the angel of the Lord, very possibly the same angel, Gabriel, that appeared to Mary and Zacharias, now began instructing Joseph in the truth of this whole perplexing matter.

Thus, the angel calls to him,

"Joseph, thou son of David!" (Matt. 1:20)

The angel first establishes the fact that Joseph is a descendant of David's royal line. Everyone knew that the Messiah of Israel would come through David.* Thus, it was necessary that the angel put this poor carpenter in mind of his high birth. He is telling him to, value yourself, Joseph, for thou art the son of David, through whom the line of the Messiah is to be drawn. *"Fear not to take unto thee Mary thy wife."* In other words, whatever doubts or reservation you may have about those things Mary told you, fear and doubt no more.

---

* Now therefore so shalt thou say unto my servant David, Thus saith the LORD of hosts, I took thee from the sheepcote, from following the sheep, to be ruler over my people, over Israel: And I was with thee whithersoever thou wentest, and have cut off all thine enemies out of thy sight, and have made thee a great name, like unto the name of the great men that are in the earth. Moreover I will appoint a place for my people Israel, and will plant them, that they may dwell in a place of their own, and move no more; neither shall the children of wickedness afflict them any more, as beforetime, and as since the time that I commanded judges to be over my people Israel, and have caused thee to rest from all thine enemies. Also the LORD telleth thee that he will make thee an house. And when thy days be fulfilled, and thou shalt sleep with thy fathers, I will set up thy seed after thee, which shall proceed out of thy bowels, and I will establish his kingdom. He shall build an house for my name, and I will establish the throne of his kingdom for ever. I will be his father, and he shall be my son. If he commit iniquity, I will chasten him with the rod of men, and with the stripes of the children of men: But my mercy shall not depart away from him, as I took it from Saul, whom I put away before thee. And thine house and thy kingdom shall be established for ever before thee: thy throne shall be established for ever. According to all these words, and according to all this vision, so did Nathan speak unto David (II Sam. 7:8-17).

> *"for that which is conceived in her IS (indeed) of the Holy Spirit" (Matt 1:20).*

> *"And she SHALL bring forth a son, and you, Joseph, SHALL call his name JESUS: for he SHALL save his people from their sins" (Matt. 1:21).*

I deliberately added the emphasis to show the way these verses seem to confirm everything that Mary would have told Joseph, as it was related to her by the angel. All doubt is removed in these emphatic statements by the angel. Yet, as though he wanted to remove every shadow of doubt, the angel continues his statement as if to explain,

> *"Now all this was done, (Joseph,) that it might be fulfilled which was spoken of the Lord by the prophet, (saying,) 'Behold, a virgin shall be with child, and shall bring forth a son, and they shall call his name Emmanuel, which being interpreted is, God with us'" (Matt. 1:22-23).*

More than seven hundred years earlier, God had promised, through His prophet Isaiah, that a great sign would be given to Israel; that a virgin would conceive and bear a son, and this child would be named Emmanuel, because in Him, God would dwell amongst men.

> *"Therefore the Lord himself shall give you a sign; Behold, a virgin shall conceive, and bear a son, and shall call his name Emmanuel" (Isaiah 7:14).*

Israel held to this promise, down through these intervening years, always wondering, much as the believer today, "Will this be the year of His Coming?" But, now, the angel is confirming to Joseph, even as he did to Mary and Elisabeth, that this conception of Mary's is, indeed, the fulfillment of that very prophecy.

So the truth that Joseph is seeking is now established in the form of a threefold witness; the witness of the angel Gabriel through Joseph's beloved Mary, the witness of the Holy Spirit through Mary's cousin Elisabeth, and the witness of the angel to Joseph directly in his dream.

Deut. 19:15 tells us that:

"... at the mouth of two witnesses, or at the mouth of three witnesses, shall the matter be established."

Thus, the matter is firmly established and Joseph now has his answer,

"...fear not to take unto thee Mary thy wife: for that which is conceived in her is (indeed) of the Holy Spirit" (Matt. 1:20).

And it is just as God had promised. The angel had completely corroborated his promises to Mary in every aspect. Mary's faith and trust in her God was completely vindicated. Even her parents now could rejoice with her in her new, exalted and blessed state.

What more can we say? Very little, indeed. The fact that the angel spoke to Joseph in a dream, and to Mary while she was awake, is of little consequence. From Mary, the Lord must have her voluntary statement of surrender and submission,

"Behold the handmaid of the Lord; be it unto me according to they word" (Luke 1:37).

So the angel must needs speak to her while she was awake. From Joseph, all God wanted was obedient action, so He spoke to him in a dream. I imagine that Joseph had lost enough sleep over this whole matter as it was, so God was gracious to speak to him while he slept, so that when he did wake up, he could take immediate action. And thus he did, for Matt. 1:24 tells us that

> *"as soon as he was raised from his sleep, Joseph did as the angel had instructed him and (immediately) took unto him his wife Mary."*

Joseph, being indeed a true son of David, and the just man that he was, manifested swift and complete obedience. The angel had reminded him of the prophecy. Thus, Joseph *"knew her not"* as his wife, *"until (after) she had brought forth her first born Son: and he (Joseph) called His name JESUS."* (Matt. 1:25).

In this total account of Mary we see a picture of the sovereign working of God in the life of an individual, who, having received the word of God from the messenger of God, believed it, simply and explicitly, and then surrendered to its commands as a true bond slave should. Then, she saw God's great performance of that work in and through her, that He had set out to do. The possible ramifications notwithstanding, she believed that God had spoken, and since she trusted Him completely, she could rest in Him, casting all her cares upon Him, knowing that He cared also for her. (Compare I Pet. 5:7)

The Church, the Body of Christ, is looking for individuals like Mary among its believers today; Christians who will follow her example, and present their bodies also, as living sacrifices, made holy by the sanctifying work of the blood of Christ; and all the while, seeing such an attitude and action as no more than their reasonable service.

> *"I beseech you therefore, brethren, by the mercies of God, that ye present your bodies a living sacrifice, holy, acceptable unto God, which is your reasonable service"* (Rom. 12:1).

Do you desire to give a gift to Jesus on His birthday? What better gift than the one Mary gave; her total being and her absolute confidence and trust? The Lord alone knows what the possible outcome of such a gift could be.

And one of the wonderful things about it is that you can give it any day of the year, even today. May it be so even now, Lord Jesus.

Chapter 3

"It Came to Pass in Those Days" (Luke 2:1)

Scripture is silent about the life of Joseph and Mary during those six months of their married life before the birth of Jesus, except to say that Joseph had no union with her until after Jesus was born. For it must be so, even as it was written,

> *"a virgin shall be with child, and (a virgin) shall bring forth a Son" (Matt. 1:23).*

This was the message of the angel of the Lord to Joseph as he dreamed, and verse 24 gives testimony to the fact that when Joseph awoke, he

> *"did as the angel of the Lord had bidden him."*

We pick up the narrative again in Luke 2:1-5 just a few days before Jesus is born.

> *"And it came to pass in those days that there went out a decree from Caesar Augustus that all the world (the whole Roman Empire) should be registered for the purpose of taxation. (This actual taxation was made when Cyrenius was governor of Syria the first time). And all went to be registered, every one to his own city. And Joseph also went up from Galilee, out of the city of Nazareth, into Judaea, unto the city of David, which is called Bethlehem; (because he was of the*

*house and lineage of David:) to be registered
(along) with Mary his espoused wife, being great
with child."*

In the first chapter of our story, we took a panoramic
look into how this particular time in all the history of
mankind was the "fullest" or "most opportune" time for
the birth of the Saviour. In this chapter, we want to take
a more detailed look at the conditions that existed "in
those days" when all this came to pass. We want to look
at just what did really happen when

*"there went out a decree from Caesar Augustus
that ALL the world, (the whole Roman Empire,)
should be registered" (Luke 2:1).*

To appreciate just what is being said here in these few
words let us take a look at both Caesar Augustus and the
Roman Empire.

"In those days" was during the time of the despotic
reign of Caesar Augustus who was the first Roman
Emperor. He was a great-nephew of Julius Caesar and his
real name was Caius Octavious. The name Augustus is
significant because that was his title. He took the name
Caesar by courtesy and by adoption from his uncle. The
title of Augustus was created especially for him by the
Roman Senate.

Originally, the Roman republic was ruled by the
people. As time went on the government was vested in
military governors called "imperators," but finally this
man, a singularly able and astute man, was able to gain
supreme power, and became the first Emperor. The word
"imperator" was a military title, but this man was the first
Imperator with a capitol "I." The generals of the Roman
republic ceased to have the title, and thus began pure
despotism and autocracy in the Roman Empire. Such
being the case what title should he take? He declined to
be called "Dictator" which suggested to him a temporary

office. He refused to be called "king" because this title didn't, so he thought, signify enough to suit him. Thus, in consultation with the Senate, this title of "Augustus" was created for him, and it indicated religious sanctions. With this title, he was on his way to the ultimate claim of deity for the supreme ruler of the Roman Empire. Thus, the Roman republic passed away and in its place emerged the Roman Empire, under Augustus Caesar.

This was a time of universal peace throughout the Empire. The doors of the Temple of Janus, which were open when the Republic was at war, had been closed for ten years or more, and remained closed for thirty years. It was "in those days" when the Roman republic had come under the despotism of an autocratic ruler; "in those days" when that autocratic ruler and that empire had bludgeoned the whole world into absolute submission, when the whole world was literally crushed under the heel of a tyrannical despot; "in those days," the one period in the history of all humanity when absolute power and world mastery was vested in one man; "in those days," Jesus was born.

"In those days," Caesar Augustus issued a decree that his whole empire, the whole world, should be registered for the purpose of taxation. AND IT WAS DONE! There was absolutely no appeal. And so they all went: Roman aristocrats in their purple splendor; Roman peasants, some of them in rags; ALL went. The high, the low, the rich, the poor, the strong, the weak, into his own city to be registered. He literally upset the whole world with this decree in preparation for levying taxation.

This registration was started under Julius Caesar, and was continued by means of this decree under Augustus. It took 32 years to complete. But what purpose did it serve?

In this registration there was recorded the name, age, profession and fortune of each head of a family, along

47

with the number, age and sex of each of his children with a view to the assessment of a "head tax."

In Syria, which included Palestine, a male individual was subject to a "head tax" from his 14th year and throughout his life. A female was taxed from her 12th year to her 60th.

The actual taxation took place under the first reign of Quirinius as governor of Syria. This taxation eventually led to the insurrection reported in Acts 5:37.

Yes, this was a time of universal peace in the Roman Empire. More correctly, it was a time of no war, but there was no peace in the hearts of the people of the realm. Instead, it was the blackest, the most damnable condition the world had ever seen. Why? Because there was no war! The people throughout the world had been clubbed into complete and absolute submission, and no man, woman, boy or girl dare peep, chirp or mutter, or even call their soul their own, because of the despot on the throne. "In those days" was the darkest hour the world has ever seen.

Now "in those days" in that Roman Empire, way down in that turbulent little bit of land at the eastern end of the Mediterranean Sea in that little land of Palestine this thing happened. There were two people there, a young man and woman, two relatively poor people among the multitudes of all Judaea, Galilee and that whole region, one couple out of all the massed multitudes of the Roman Empire, yea, of the whole world. These two people had no more influence on Caesar Augustus and the Roman Empire than any relatively poor, newly wed couple in this country might have on our President. So far as their earthly estate was concerned, they were totally insignificant. Yet, they were touched by this Roman authority. This decree of Caesar Augustus reached their little town of Nazareth and Joseph must obey. Even though the royal blood of Israel's king David coursed through Joseph's veins he must bow his neck with the rest and go up to register. There was no appeal. He can't send someone else in his place. HE must go to the city of his family and register. So he went, and Mary, who was also of the house and lineage of David went with him, and she was great with child. Two people, and few others except possibly some of their closest friends knew anything about them, and they knew very little. This is the picture the world saw and that was all they saw.

But look again. For things are seldom as they seem. There is Mary, and in her womb is tabernacled the very Son of God, the Saviour of all mankind from the beginning to the end of time. And with her is Joseph, his one concern and passion is to guard and protect this woman and her precious Burden.

In our minds let us climb even higher and try to look on this total drama from heaven's vantage point. So far as the world was concerned they were traveling the 65 miles or so from Nazareth of Galilee to Bethlehem of Judaea because Caesar Augustus had at that precise moment in history issued his decree that all the world would be enrolled. That decree of Caesar Augustus traveled across the world, touching every person, and Joseph and Mary were no exception. The world would say that Caesar Augustus is master of all the world, and Mary and Joseph are poor innocent victims of this tyrant's whims. But look again now from this heavenly vantage point. Back in the Old Testament of my Bible in the little book of Micah, I read a prophecy of God written over six hundred fifty years before this event even happened; written before those refugees from Troy had even established a government in the small, scattered village on the banks of the Tiber River that eventually became the city, and later the Empire of Rome. And it says,

> **"But thou, Bethlehem Ephratah, though thou be little among the thousands of Judah, yet out of thee shall He come forth unto me that is to be**

49

> *Ruler in Israel; Whose goings forth are from of old, from everlasting. Therefore will He give them up until the time that she who travaileth hath brought forth; then the remnant of His brethren shall return unto the children of Israel" (Micah 5:2-3).*

Where, according to this prophecy, was this One Who was to be Ruler of all Israel to be born? In Bethlehem. And where were Joseph and Mary making their home? In Nazareth of Galilee, some 65 miles due north of Bethlehem.

> *"When Herod the king had heard these things (from the Wise Men), he was troubled, and all Jerusalem with him. And when he had gathered all the chief priests and scribes of the people together, he demanded of them where Christ should be born. And they said unto him, in Bethlehem of Judah, "FOR THUS IT IS WRITTEN BY THE PROPHETS" (Matthew 2:3-5).*

And they went on to quote Micah 5:2-3.

These chief priests and scribes knew where the Messiah was to be born, even as all the holy men of Israel did, because the prophet penned these words under the inspiration and direction of the Spirit of God. Thus, they testified, whether they realized it or not, that since this thing was done in fulfillment of prophecy it was done under the government of God.

From the world's limited point of view it was Caesar Augustus who was calling the shots. But from our heavenly vantage point, we can see that all of the time God was in complete control. It didn't bother Him one iota to literally upset the entire world in order to see to it that these two people traveled the 65 or so miles necessary for Jesus' birth to take place where His prophet said it would. Surely, as Jesus Himself said,

"Till heaven and earth pass, one jot or one tittle shall in no wise pass from the law, till ALL be fulfilled" (Matthew 5:18).

How obvious it is now that the really insignificant person in this whole magnificent drama was Caesar Augustus, that little puppet in the city on the seven hills. The truly significant personalities were Mary, whose womb tabernacled the very Son of God, and Joseph, who watched over and cared for her so faithfully. That prophecy in Micah 5:4 said that this Man who was to be born in Bethlehem

"shall be great unto the ends of the earth."

Jesus **IS** coming again to re-establish the kingdom of His father David, and when He does, and only then, will the world know a truly great world Leader.

And so it was "in those days" when subjugation and great darkness was over all the earth that this great Light broke forth unto all men as this stupendous event took place.

"And so it was, that, while they were there, the days were accomplished that she should be delivered. And she brought forth her firstborn Son, and wrapped Him in swaddling clothes, and laid Him in a manger; because there was no room for them in the inn" (Luke 2:7).

Again, we get a view of the conditions in Bethlehem "in those days." *"There was no room for them in the inn."*

In our western, modern way of thinking, we immediately picture this "inn" as some sort of a hotel, or rooming place. Indeed, whenever we hear a message on this particular passage, or see a Christmas pageant, invariably this is the scene that is presented with the surly inn keeper and all the trimmings. But such was not the case.

In the New Testament the word "inn" occurs only twice, and in both instances it appears in the book of Luke. The first is this passage in Luke 2:7 and the other is in Luke 10:34. In this second reference, the Greek word is "pandocheion," and it does mean a caravansary or a hotel-like establishment. It is a place with a host (innkeeper), food and provisions, often for both the traveler and his mount if he has one. There are apartments or rooms for rent, and sometimes there is even entertainment often provided by the guests themselves. In many respects it would be similar to our hotels in early America.

But the Greek word in our passage here in Luke 2:7 is not "pandocheion" but "kataluma." This inn is quite a different arrangement altogether. It is merely a walled enclosure, a sheepfold open to the sky, into which travelers or shepherds might drive their flocks for protection for the night. At this place, along the sides there were sometimes inns or covered rooms where the drovers could bed down and rest, after their cattle were secure within the walls. There was water, but no food, for either the men or their flocks. No host and no entertainment. There was room here for the cattle, but no room for this weary couple with their precious Burden. How dark this hour was.

What could they do? This time for Mary is a supreme hour that will not permit delays, and something must be done quickly. So, they turn to the cattle feeding areas on the edge of town. Sometimes these were a sort of "out building," crudely constructed and positioned to protect the feeding mangers from the weather. It was to such a place as this that Mary and Joseph resorted, and it was here that Mary gave birth to the baby Jesus, attended only by Joseph.

Our passage could be read, *"and* **SHE** *brought forth her firstborn Son, and* **SHE** *wrapped Him in swaddling clothing, and* **SHE** *laid Him in the cattle feeding trough."* Even though she was cast upon herself, and such help as Joseph could be to her, still, this verse literally abounds in peace as one reads it. If ever the truth of Deuteronomy 31:6 has been demonstrated in its fullest meaning, it was demonstrated here by Mary.

> *"Be strong and of a good courage, fear not, nor be afraid.. for the Lord thy God, He it is that doth go with thee; He will not fail thee, nor forsake thee" (Deut. 31:6).*

In concluding this chapter I think of all the possible places Jesus might have been born. But they were passed up in the Divine Providence so that Jesus would be born into this fantastically low and humble setting. Here in a cattle feeding area on the edge of this little, insignificant village of Bethlehem, the King of kings, the Lord of lords, the Great High Priest of all times, the Saviour of all mankind of all ages was born.

Surely, such a King, the promised Son of King David of old would be born in a palace. The Wise Men who came to Jerusalem bearing their gifts for "Him who is born King of the Jews," looked for Him in the palace at Jerusalem. But no, God in His wisdom passed up the king's palace. Then, if not the King born in a palace, surely the Lord of lords would be born in the lavish home of one of the Lords or Elders of Israel of that day. But such was not to be the case. Even for the One born to be the Heavenly Great High Priest (Hebrews 4:14), there were no provisions for Him in the Priestly quarters of the Temple. Mary and Joseph would pass these by also. One might think, too, that since Joseph and Mary were both of the house and lineage of David, which had its recognized center in Bethlehem, the city of David, surely one of them would have had some relative living there who would receive them, but

53

apparently such was not the case. They passed up this possibility also.

They passed by the caravansary, the hotel-type inns, probably for want of money to pay for their lodging. They passed up the protection of the sheep fold because there was room for only rude cattle and their drovers. There was no room to receive the Lamb of God. Finally, in that hour that would breach no further delays, they resorted to the cattle feeding areas on the edge of town, protected against the weather, to make Mary as comfortable as possible, as the Son of the Highest, the Very God of Very God makes His entrance upon this earthly scene.

How lowly this birth was. No man was ever born into a more lowly situation. Yet, this is describing the birth of the King of kings, the Lord of lords, the Saviour of all mankind of all ages. Fantastic! But why so very, very low?

No baby, born into this world, ever experienced a more lowly birth than the Baby Jesus. The circumstances surrounding His entrance into this world, there amidst the stench and filth of the animals that frequented this feeding area, with only the leftover hay or fodder as bedding for either Mary or the Baby, were as debasing as those circumstances that accompanied His death.

But really, in Divine Providence, such must be the case. For now He was born low enough that He could reach down and save any other man born of woman, regardless of that person's economic or social status in life.

So it was in this setting, as Luke tells us

"That the days were accomplished that Mary should be delivered"

of her precious burden.

"And she brought forth her firstborn Son, wrapped Him in swaddling clothes, and laid Him

in a manger, (or crib for fodder) because there was no room for Him in the (kataluma,)" (Luke 2:6-7)

the usual place for the shelter of sheep. Thus it was that the Lamb of God was born outside the sheepfold so that in God's appointed time He might bring us back into the Fold of God.

CHAPTER 4

"And She Brought Forth Her Firstborn Son."

> *"And Mary brought forth her firstborn Son and wrapped Him in swaddling clothes and laid Him in a manger, because there was no room for them in the sheepfold type of inn" (free translation)(Luke. 2:7).*

I have always gotten a real blessing and much enlightenment from word studies in the Bible, and there are two more words in this verse that need looking into in order to get a better grasp of the truth surrounding the birth of Jesus. They are the words "firstborn" and "swaddling clothes."

"Firstborn" is the Greek noun "prototokos," and it occurs in the New Testament nine different times, translated in the King James text either as "first begotten" or "firstborn." There is no question that in this Luke 2:7 passage, and again in Matthew 1:25, both of which deal with the actual birth of Jesus, the word means "firstborn in order of events." Jesus was the first child born to Mary, because His was a "virgin birth."

Matthew 13:55-56 tells us:

> *"Is not this the carpenter's son? is not his mother called Mary? and his brethren, James, and Joses, and Simon, and Judas? And his sisters, are they*

57

not all with us? Whence then hath this man all these things?"

These verses point out that Mary and Joseph had at least four other sons and two daughters after Jesus was born, so Jesus was the firstborn in point of time and in order of events. In each of the other usages of this Greek word in the New Testament, it has no reference to time or order of events, but rather, it shows Jesus as the Pre-eminent One, the Chief One, or the One with authority to rule. Jacob's blessing of his firstborn son, Reuben, is as good a description of this word "prototokos" as there is in the Bible.

"Reuben, thou art my firstborn, my might, and the beginning of my strength, the excellency of dignity, and the excellency of power" (Genesis 49:3).

So, not only did Mary bring forth her "Firstborn in order of events," but He was also her "Firstborn in His Pre-eminence" in His own family, and in the family of mankind.

Then our passage, Lk. 2:7, tells us that Mary wrapped the Baby Jesus

"in swaddling clothes and laid Him in a manger."

The descriptions I have heard as to just what "swaddling clothes" are leave much to be desired for accuracy, especially in light of the customs of the Eastern culture of that day.

A passage in Ezekiel 16:4 sheds more light on this term "swaddling clothes" where we read (speaking to Israel of that day):

"And as for thy nativity, in the day that thou was born thy navel was not cut, neither wast thou

*washed in water to supple thee; thou wast not
salted at all, nor swaddled at all."*

All of this, of course, has reference to the childbirth
customs practiced in Israel. After the baby was born it was
cleaned up carefully, its navel tied and trimmed; then
immediately a tiny bit of salt was rubbed on the baby to
indicate that the parents intended to teach the child to be
truthful and good to his word, a person to be trusted. In
this way the parents and the child came under a
"covenant of salt" with God.

After this salting the baby was wrapped in "swaddling
clothes." These were usually fine linen strips, not rags as
some have said, but much like roll bandages of our day.
These strips were wrapped around the baby's body to
straighten him out. His body, including his arms and legs,
was made as straight as a ramrod. This rite was a sign to
God that the parents would rear the child to be
straightforward before the Lord and man, and free from
all crookedness.

The child was left in this condition for a period of from
fifteen minutes to two hours during which time the
parents meditated and made their vows to God
concerning the sacred trust given them when they
received the child. This same ancient tradition is still
practiced in certain areas in the Orient today, and
regardless of how expensive the baby's layette may be, the
"swaddling clothes" are used to depict this covenant with
God.

So, Mary wrapped her firstborn baby, Jesus, in just such
"swaddling clothes" in keeping with the ancient
tradition. She then undoubtedly laid Him on the fodder
or hay in one of the mangers in this feeding area which
was located on the outskirts of the village of Bethlehem
where they had taken refuge as a last resort.

Oh the pity of it...the pathos...the tragedy and loneliness of it, that in this hour of all hours, when womanhood should be surrounded by the tenderest care, Mary was alone, cast upon herself except for what little help Joseph might be to her at this time. But Dr. Luke is careful and very distinct in writing about this night. Mary, with her own hands, wrapped the baby Jesus round and round with those swaddling bands and laid Him in his manger bed. There was no one to do it for her. And thus the Son of God in human form had entered the stream of human history. The Firstborn of all creation:

"Who is the image of the invisible God, the firstborn of every creature" (Colossians 1:15);

the Firstborn from among the dead:

"And he is the head of the body, the church: who is the beginning, the firstborn from the dead; that in all things he might have the preeminence." (Colossians 1:18);

the Firstborn of many brethren:

"For whom he did foreknow, he also did predestinate to be conformed to the image of his Son, that he might be the firstborn among many brethren" (Romans 8:29).

Indeed, Mary not only brought forth her Firstborn, but, at the same time she brought forth God's Firstborn, the Eternal Son of God. And she tenderly wrapped Him in those swaddling bands and laid Him in a manger.

So the purpose for which the angel Gabriel had come to Mary, seeking the use of her body by the Holy Spirit of God that He might produce His Fruit in her, had been fulfilled.

This indeed was a lonely, difficult hour for Mary, but once again, God had shown Himself faithful, and more than adequate to the situation. Mary's every need was cared for. If not in the usual manner, it was in the miraculous provision of physical and spiritual strength for Mary and the Baby in this time of greatest need.

And, while the circumstances of Mary, Joseph and the Baby in the place of this birth, there in the cattle feeding area on the outskirts of Bethlehem were, to say the least, unusual, so were the circumstances that presented themselves to others, both in the immediate area and also, many, many miles away. For we read in Luke 2:8 that at the time of Jesus' birth, the fact of His birth was being proclaimed to certain shepherds in the area who were guarding their flocks on the Judean hillside. And then in Matthew 2:2 the Wise Men proclaim the fact that they also had seen the Baby's star many miles away in the East. We will study these men in a later chapter.

One other interesting point should be mentioned here, and that is the fact that the Great Pyramid of Egypt, as though it were being informed beforehand to get ready for the young Child who was ultimately to come there for refuge, in its own way saw the revelation of Jesus' birth in the heavens.

In a study of this pyramid, one finds that from deep within the bowels of this fantastic structure, there is a very long viewing shaft, or opening, that looks out upon the heavens. Because of its great length, and the darkness inside the pyramid, any time one looks out through this viewing passage, whether day or night, one can see the stars of heaven that are lined up with the passage at that time.

Astronomers have calculated, as only they can do, that at the time of Jesus' birth the constellation LAMB was lined up exactly with that viewing passage. Thus, the stars of the heavens declared to the inner recesses of that great pyramid that the birth of

61

"the Lamb of God which taketh away the sin of the world," (John 1:29)

had indeed come to pass.

Psalm 19:1 tells us that

"the heavens declare the glory of God."

So it was on this night of nights, for the One through Whom God was to reveal everything that man could possibly know about Himself was born. The Glory of God in the Person of His only begotten Son was being declared near and far, high and low.

So, Mary and Joseph may have found themselves in very humble surroundings, in certainly a less than desirable setting, at a very frightening time in their lives, in an out-of- the-way place on the edge of the City of David; but this did not hinder God from making clear to all the world the miracle that had happened there that night.

Yet, equally amazing is God's choice of the ones to whom He would first reveal the fulfillment of this prophecy. To shepherds? Of all the people He could have chosen...the king, the priests, the lords of Israel, why in the world would God choose shepherds? Many have speculated on this choice, but several things do come to mind as we study the passages in Luke that speak of this revelation to the shepherds.

The account begins in Luke 2:8 where we read:

"And there were in the same country, shepherds abiding in the field, keeping watch over their flock by night."

Notice that it was "in the same country," (the area around Bethlehem), that these shepherds were living in the fields with their sheep as they watched over them and it was night.

It has been generally established that the wording of this verse has reference to the "temple shepherds" who were assigned to watch over the flocks intended for the "temple sacrifices." These were normally pastured in the country around Bethlehem, only about seven miles south of the temple site in Jerusalem. The sacrificial animals always had to be prefect specimens without spot or blemish, so they required careful watching over to see that they came to no harm or injury that would render them unusable. Also, it has been the custom from time immemorial for shepherds to live in the fields with their flocks during lambing time, and many believe that this was the reason these shepherds were living in the field at this particular time.

And it was at night. Natural darkness had settled over the area, as if to emphasize the spiritual darkness that had likewise settled over the world of that day. Such was the darkness that greeted the Son of God at His birth. Such was the darkness that He had come to dispel. It was into this dark setting that the Lord's angel came to witness to these shepherds that a Saviour, the Messiah of Israel, had indeed been born. The One that every animal sacrifice pointed forward to had been born in the City of David.

Picture the setting if you can, and try to appreciate the fantastic element of surprise. The shepherds had made their bivouac, and they were now in the darkness of night when the sheep would usually be settled. Some of the shepherds would undoubtedly have been sleeping, while others kept their watch, warming themselves at the low fire, and talking about nothing in particular, just keeping each other company. Suddenly,

"the angel of the Lord" (the Lord's angel), "appeared in their midst, and the Glory of the Lord" (the same shekinah glory that had filled

the tabernacle of old). "shone round about them: and they were exceedingly fearful" (free translation) (Luke 2:9).

But this was not a time for fear. It was a time for rejoicing...for thanksgiving and praise...a time for the telling of good news. So the angel spoke to them, even as he had to Mary nine months before, to first of all dispel their fears and set their hearts at ease. The angel told them the reason they should have no fear.

"For, behold, I bring you good tidings of great joy, which shall be to all people. For unto you is born this day in the City of David a Saviour which is Messiah the Lord" (Luke 2:10-11).

And then, as if the angel knew that the natural response of these shepherds would be to go and try to find this Baby, this Lamb of God, he went on to tell them all they needed to know to identify Jesus, once they found Him.

And thus, the angel continued, saying,

"And this shall be a sign unto you; you shall find the Babe wrapped in His swaddling bands and lying in a cattle feeding trough" (Luke 2:12).

What more sure identification could they possibly want? There certainly wasn't more than one such situation as this (a new born infant wrapped in swaddling bands and lying in a cattle feeding trough), in the little City of David. There wasn't a situation like this anywhere else in the world. This is the type of positive identification I would have needed.

And then, as if the heavens could no longer restrain their joy and praise, their declaring of the glory of God who had just been born, Luke tells us that:

"Suddenly, there was with this one angel, a whole multitude of heavenly hosts, praising God and saying," (literally), "Glory to God in the highest heaven, and on earth peace to men with whom He is pleased" (Luke 2:13-14).

The scene here is one where the angel of the Lord is standing in the midst of the shepherds, in the strange and new light of the shekinah glory of God. He labors to dispel their unbelievable terror of fear with the good news that the promised Messiah of Israel, the Saviour of the world, had indeed been born just a few miles away in the little city of David. On top of all this, in another fantastic surprise, a very great multitude of the armies of heaven (see II Kings 6:17) burst suddenly upon this scene. This great host of Heavenly beings were all shouting praises to God at the same time, and saying, *"Glory to God in the highest heavens,"* for truly, He who dwells in the Highest Heaven is worthy of ALL glory, from every corner of His creation. They were also shouting and proclaiming that on earth there should be

"peace among those men with whom God was pleased" (Luke 2:14).

The angel had already told the shepherds that there was born this day in the city of David, a Saviour, and it was this Saviour who would ultimately make it possible for God and man to be reconciled.

Romans 5:10 tells us:

"For if, when we were enemies we were reconciled to God by the death of His Son, much more being reconciled, we shall be saved by His life."

For unregenerate man, there is no peace, because he is still an enemy of God...still in his trespasses and sins. Isaiah 48:22 underscores this truth when he writes:

65

"There is no peace, saith the Lord, unto the wicked."

But in that little town of Bethlehem this night, was born the Son of God...that One who would make it possible for wicked men, who were the enemies of God, to be reconciled to God. Thus, they would not only lose that designation, "enemies of God," but, at the same time, they would be regenerated to the position of a member of the family of God, the Body of Christ, as sons with *the* Son. In this way they would become those with whom God could be pleased, and thus come to know the peace of which this great multitude from the armies of heaven spoke.

The term, "heavenly host," of which there was such a great multitude, stirred my curiosity to know just who they were. We know from Luke 2:15 that these heavenly hosts were angelic beings. Yet, I was reminded of that passage in II Kings 6:13-17 where Elisha, the man of God, being in the city of Dothan, was surrounded by the hosts of his enemy, the king of Syria.

"And he said, Go and spy where he is, that I may send and fetch him. And it was told him, saying, Behold, he is in Dothan. Therefore sent he thither horses, and chariots, and a great host: and they came by night, and compassed the city about. And when the servant of the man of God was risen early, and gone forth, behold, an host compassed the city both with horses and chariots. And his servant said unto him, Alas, my master! how shall we do? And he answered, Fear not: for they that be with us are more than they that be with them. And Elisha prayed, and said, LORD, I pray thee, open his eyes, that he may see. And the LORD opened the eyes of the young man; and he saw: and, behold, the mountain was full

of horses and chariots of fire round about Elisha"
(II Kings 6:13-17).

In this situation, Elisha's young servant became fearful and asked his master, *"Alas, what are we going to do?"* It was at this point that Elisha prayed, and asked God to reveal to this young man the unseen hosts or armies of heaven that surrounded not only these faithful servants of God, but also they surrounded the enemies of these servants of God. They consisted of *"horses and chariots of fire."* In this particular instance, it says that the servant of Elisha saw that the mountain was *"full"* of these hosts of heaven.

Anyone who has done any serious study of the Bible at all soon becomes aware that there is a great battle going on between the forces of evil under the leadership of Satan and the forces of righteousness under the leadership of God. This battle originated before the creation of man when the Archangel Lucifer rebelled against God and attempted to take over authority from God, but was ultimately thrown out of heaven. (Compare Isaiah 14:12-17 and Ezekiel 28:12-15).

To this day this battle continues to rage....

"Finally, my brethren, be strong in the Lord, and in the power of his might. Put on the whole armour of God, that ye may be able to stand against the wiles of the devil. For we wrestle not against flesh and blood, but against principalities, against powers, against the rulers of the darkness of this world, against spiritual wickedness in high places. Wherefore take unto you the whole armour of God, that ye may be able to withstand in the evil day, and having done all, to stand. Stand therefore, having your loins girt about with truth, and having on the breastplate of righteousness; And your feet shod with the

> *preparation of the gospel of peace; Above all,*
> *taking the shield of faith, wherewith ye shall be*
> *able to quench all the fiery darts of the wicked.*
> *And take the helmet of salvation, and the sword*
> *of the Spirit, which is the word of God" (Eph.*
> *6:10-17).*

....and it will continue, until Satan is finally cast into the "bottomless pit" in accordance with Biblical prophecy.

Throughout the various campaigns of this battle Satan has attempted to thwart God's plan for the salvation of mankind by destroying the line through which the Saviour was to come. In at least one point of history this line was reduced to one person, an infant child. But Satan was never able to eliminate the line completely. Thus it is that both Mary and Joseph could trace their family trees all the way back to Abraham, the one to whom the specific promise of the Saviour was given. They could even go back to Adam, as is indicated in Luke 3. Joseph's line is shown in Matthew 1:1-16, while Mary's lineage is recorded in Luke 3:23-38. Because of these attempts by Satan to destroy the royal line of David, and because no mention is made of the parents of Mary or Joseph in the New Testament (except as the names of their fathers appear in the two genealogies), some commentators surmise that it was possible that both Mary and Joseph were orphans, the very last of the two lines back to King David. This cannot be established as biblical truth, but it would not have been beyond Satan to have tried to eliminate the lines at this point as he tried in the past.

Now I have mentioned all this to point out that Satan would stop at nothing to prevent Jesus from going to the Cross, because it was Jesus' death on the Cross that sealed Satan's doom. So, if Satan was ever going to stop Jesus from fulfilling His ultimate ministry what better time than when He lay so helpless and vulnerable there on His manger bed, clothed only in swaddling bands, and barely protected from the elements over which Satan rules as prince?

We know from scripture that at numerous times Satan would have had Jesus destroyed if he could, but his every effort was thwarted. So who better could look after the protection of the infant Child and the helpless parents than the armies of heaven with their horses and chariots of fire, just as they did Elisha and his young servant, almost 900 years before?

Mary and Joseph and the others of Bethlehem may not have known they were there, but God knew it, Satan knew it, and that is all that makes any difference. By God's grace their presence was also revealed to the shepherds as it was to the young servant of Elisha to encourage their hearts to believe that God was indeed again working in Israel. But as these hosts of the armies of heaven kept their vigil over the Christ Child that night they could not hold back their shouts of praise to God for His unspeakable gift any longer. Suddenly, as a gigantic clap of thunder, it came rolling forth over the Judean hillside, to add to the total wonder the shepherds experienced that night.

But soon the angels departed from their midst and they were left to ponder what this experience could mean. Then with little hesitation they agreed between themselves to leave the tending of the temple sheep chosen for the sacrificial offerings and go to Bethlehem and see this thing which had come to pass. So even though it was lambing time on the Judean hillside, a time when the shepherds lived right in the midst of their flocks, they must now go. They left these shadow sacrifices to see this wondrous Baby, the One great Sacrifice to end all sacrifices. The Lamb of God was being born. Who could better tend to him than the shepherds designated to look after the sacrificial lambs of God?

So they hurried to Bethlehem, and as the angel had said, they found Mary and Joseph. And sure enough there was the Baby wrapped in His swaddling bands lying in the cattle feeding trough.

We aren't told of any meeting of the shepherds and Wise Men (the Magi), yet they are often pictured together. Also, we aren't told of any conversation that went on between the parents and the shepherds, for who could speak anything in the face of what they saw? Such wonder, such glory, and yet, here was the Son of God, the Greater Son of King David, the promised Messiah of Israel, lying in this rude manger bed amidst the squalor of the animals that frequented this place. He was protected from the elements only by the protection usually afforded the fodder for the animals. The total scene is unbelievable. Yet thus it was that Mary brought forth her firstborn son.

Once the shepherds had seen the Baby, this Lamb of God, and were assured that He was being cared for properly, they left the manger scene and immediately began to proclaim everything that was told them by the angels concerning this child. Once again, God chooses such unlikely prospects as these rude shepherds to be the first evangelists of the Lord's Christ. God does indeed work in mysterious ways His wonders and His works to perform. The important thing was not who bore the message, but what the messengers said.

As the shepherds spread abroad throughout the night their wondrous evangel of love and peace we are told that those who heard it wondered at those things which were told them by the shepherds. It doesn't say that they believed, or rejoiced, or praised God for what they were told, they merely wondered, held in awe, or admired what they heard. Here again we get some idea of the spiritual deadness that existed in Israel at that time. And it is much the same today.

But Mary carefully kept, or remembered well, all these things and as the days went by she pondered them in her heart. That is, she meditated on them, turning them over and over in her mind as she tried to understand what it all meant. This same expression occurs again in Luke 2:51 concerning Jesus' appearance in the temple at age 12.

"And he went down with them, and came to Nazareth, and was subject unto them: but his mother kept all these sayings in her heart" (Luke 2:51).

It is interesting that we have these two references to Mary's careful remembering of these things for it is Mary who conveyed them to Dr. Luke, so that we could study them now.

Then as the shepherds returned to their work of tending the temple flocks they went in an attitude of

"praise and glory to God for everything they had heard and seen, even as it was told unto them by the angels" (Luke 2:20).

I am reminded in closing this chapter of something Peter wrote in his second epistle (II Peter 1:15-19). To summarize, Peter said that even though the disciples were eyewitnesses of His majesty, they had actually heard the Father say as they stood there on the mount of transfiguration:

"This is my beloved Son in whom I am well pleased" (II Peter 1:17 & Matthew 17:1-8).

Even though there were many other things that the disciples heard and saw that Peter could have enumerated, yet he went on to conclude that we who hold the Word of God, the Bible, in our hands, and have the indwelling Holy Spirit to interpret it to us, we have a more sure Word of Prophecy, a better revelation of the truth than these first hand, eyewitness accounts that he spoke of.

The shepherds heard and saw. The disciples heard and saw. Both were eyewitnesses. But you and I, in the Bible, have the more excellent revelation. Both the shepherds and the disciples glorified and praised God for their "second best" eyewitness accounts. What are we doing about our more excellent Word of prophecy? Are we, like Mary, remembering it well, and turning it over and over in our minds to learn as much as we can of its meaning and truth? Or are we like those in and around Bethlehem who heard the shepherds' message, and merely wondered at what this Word has said?

CHAPTER 5

"Born of a Woman, Born Under the Law"

Eight days have now passed during which time we are not told exactly what transpired in the life of this little family. Undoubtedly, Joseph was busy trying to find a better place for Mary and the Baby to stay as she recuperated and as they both gained strength. We have no reason to believe that they spent more than one night in the cattle feeding area on the edge of this little city of Bethlehem, but we are not told where they did stay. Then there was the matter of the registration ordered by Caesar Augustus. Joseph would be seeing to this, also.

We now continue the account of the birth of Jesus, and the first few days of His life in Luke 2:21 where we read,

> *"And when eight days were passed, at the time of the circumcising of the child, His name was called JESUS, the name given Him by the angel before He was conceived in the womb."*

Here again we see the character of Jesus' earthly father, Joseph, *"being a just man."* That is, as a strict observer of the Law of Moses and the Levitical Code, he was faithful to follow through in every prescribed detail of the Law. Thus, on the eighth day, as the Law instructed (Lev 12:3), Jesus was circumcised. This was a rite performed sometimes by the priest, and sometimes by the father.

73

This was the case when Abraham circumcised his own son of promise, Isaac.

> *"And Abraham circumcised his son Isaac being eight days old, as God had commanded him"* *(Gen 21:4).*

At other times, a father might invite a dear friend to help him in the performing of this rite of circumcision, and often there was a feast of celebration that accompanied the rite. It was considered a joyous occasion. Such is the picture that is given us of the circumcision of John, called the Baptist, in Luke 1:57-66. The numerous usage of the terms "they" and "all they" indicate the presence of a sizable party.

It is in the presence of this company of friends, relatives and neighbors that the name given to the baby was announced, and so it was with the Baby Jesus. Mary had been instructed what the Child was to be named even before she offered her body to the Holy Spirit for His use. In Luke 1:31 we read that the angel said unto her,

> *"And behold, thou shalt conceive in thy womb, and bring forth a Son, and shalt call his name JESUS."*

And lest there be any confusion in the matter, the same instructions were given to Joseph by the angel that spoke to him in his dream. After the angel had confirmed Mary's account of what the angel Gabriel had told her, he said unto Joseph, who, as the earthly father would have the final say.

> *"And she shall bring forth a Son and you shall call His name JESUS, for He shall save His people from their sins"* *(Mat 1:21).*

Both the circumcision and the naming of Jesus are significant. By the rite of circumcision a male baby born to a Hebrew family actually came under the covenant of promise given to Abraham:

"And God said unto Abraham, Thou shalt keep my covenant therefore, thou, and thy seed after thee in their generations. This is my covenant, which ye shall keep, between me and you and thy seed after thee; Every man child among you shall be circumcised. And ye shall circumcise the flesh of your foreskin; and it shall be a token of the covenant betwixt me and you. And he that is eight days old shall be circumcised among you, every man child in your generations, he that is born in the house, or bought with money of any stranger, which is not of thy seed. He that is born in thy house, and he that is bought with thy money, must needs be circumcised: and my covenant shall be in your flesh for an everlasting covenant. And the uncircumcised man child whose flesh of his foreskin is not circumcised, that soul shall be cut off from his people; he hath broken my covenant" (Gen 17:9-14).

Thus, through His circumcision, the Baby Jesus became a member of the nation of Israel and the Israelites became His people. Then, the name JESUS, which means literally "JEHOVAH IS SALVATION" was given to Him, because as the angel told Joseph, *"He shall save His people from their sins."*

So it was that Jesus, the Son of God, who was

"made of a woman, made under the law," (Gal 4:4-5)

became subject to that law in every respect,

"To redeem them that were under the law, that we (you and I) might receive the adoption of sons" (Gal 4:4-5).

75

Joseph, "being a just man," also would have looked after the careful recording of this rite of circumcision and the naming of the Child so that the genealogy records kept in the temple were accurate in every detail. Thus it was no problem for Dr. Luke or Matthew to read the genealogy of Christ all the way back to Adam, either through Mary's line as recorded in Luke 3:23-38, or through Joseph's line as recorded in Matthew 1:1-18.

Now so far as the birth of Christ is concerned the account could be considered complete at this point. Jesus was born, He was officially introduced to the nation of Israel through the rite of circumcision, and His name was properly recorded under the tribe of Judah, as a new member of the Jewish community. But since the Christmas story usually continues up to the point of the first of the silent years, the point where the young family returns from Egypt to the little community of Nazareth, I would like to follow the account to that point in this study also.

We pick up the account again in Luke's Gospel at chapter 2:22:

"And when the days of her (Mary's) purification according to the law of Moses were accomplished, they (Mary and Joseph) brought Him to Jerusalem to present Him to the Lord; (as it is written in the law of the Lord, every male that openeth the womb shall be called holy to the Lord); and to offer a sacrifice according to that which is said in the law of the Lord, a pair of turtle doves or two young pigeons."

There are several points that need to be cleared up here to help us understand just how the story actually progressed. First of all, it was a requirement of the Mosaic law that a certain number of days had to pass before the new mother could make the required sacrificial offerings

76

to complete the rite of her purification. These requirements are spelled out in Leviticus 12:2-8, and say basically that forty days of purification were required for a male child, and eighty days for a female.

Then the law actually provided that to conclude the rite of purification two offerings were to be brought to the priest at the temple door. A yearling lamb was to be sacrificed as a burnt-offering unto the Lord, and either a young pigeon or a turtle dove as a sin-offering. But, if the family was poor and could not afford the yearling lamb, provision was made in the law that they could substitute two turtle doves or two young pigeons, one for the burnt-offering, and the other for the sin-offering.

These requirements indicate that it was forty days after the birth of Jesus that Mary and Joseph came to the temple to present Him to the Lord, and that they obviously were of limited means because they offered sacrifices for Mary's purification in accordance with the provisions in the Law for the poor.

Since they came to Jerusalem at the end of the forty days, apparently they had remained in Bethlehem during this early period of Jesus' life. We are not told just where they lived at this time, but it could have been at the home of a relative of either Joseph or Mary since both of them were of the house and lineage of David, and Bethlehem was David's city. Time would have been available to Joseph to look up such relatives after Jesus' birth that was not available to him in the urgency of the hour that marked their arrival. During this time I am sure they would have re-established old family ties, and celebrated with old and new friends the rite of circumcision and the naming of the new Baby. Mary would have rested, while she and the Baby Jesus both gained the much needed strength they would require for the trip back to Nazareth.

But now the required forty days have passed. The registration required by Caesar Augustus has been taken care of, and Mary and Joseph bid farewell to their hosts in Bethlehem, to begin the trek back to Nazareth. But, since Jerusalem is on the route home, they must first visit the temple to fulfill all the requirements of the Mosaic law concerning both Mary and the Baby Jesus. So Jesus is brought into the temple where He, as the firstborn male child, must be presented unto the Lord.

"For I will pass through the land of Egypt this night, and will smite all the firstborn in the land of Egypt, both man and beast; and against all the gods of Egypt I will execute judgment: I am the LORD. And the blood shall be to you for a token upon the houses where ye are: and when I see the blood, I will pass over you, and the plague shall not be upon you to destroy you, when I smite the land of Egypt" (Ex. 12:12-13).

"For all the firstborn of the children of Israel are mine, both man and beast: on the day that I smote every firstborn in the land of Egypt I sanctified them for myself" (Num 8:17).

And so it was that as they entered the temple,

"...to do for Him after the custom of the law," (Luke 2:24)

they were met by Simeon, the man of God.

Simeon is one of the more interesting of the lesser known personalities of the New Testament. He is not mentioned before or after these few verses in Luke 2, but these verses do tell us quite a lot about the man. He holds no apparent office in the temple, but he is truly a man of God. Luke 2:25 tells us that he was both *"just and devout."* Remember that Jesus' earthly father, Joseph, was referred to as

"a just man" (Matt 1:19).

In the case of Simeon, the two terms *"just and devout"* combine to indicate the righteousness of the individual, his right standing before God. He is called *"just"* because he was justified before God. He had faithfully performed all the requirements of the Law for his sins and offered in faith the required sacrifices. It was because of his unwavering faith in the propitiary nature of these sacrifices and their ultimate consummation in the promised Messiah, that he was said to be *"devout."* Compare the similar description of Zacharias and Elisabeth, the father and mother of John the Baptist:

"And they were both righteous before God, walking in all the commandments and ordinances of the Lord blameless" (Luke 1:6).

Luke goes on to tell us that Simeon

"waited for the consolation of Israel" (Luke 2:25).

This term "consolation of Israel" is really just another title for the Messiah of Israel. The Amplified New Testament, in translating this phrase, capitalizes the word "Consolation" to bring this idea out more clearly. So, what the phrase is actually saying is that Simeon was waiting for the promised Messiah. We will come back to this thought just a little later.

We also read in Luke 2:25 that the Holy Spirit* was *upon* Him. Throughout the Old Testament economy, which actually includes the four Gospels and much of the Acts, we read where the Spirit of God comes upon, or fills certain chosen individuals for some specific ministry. But nowhere in the Old Testament, or the Gospels, is the Holy Spirit described as indwelling an individual as is the case

---

* (The koine Greek word for "ghost" does not appear in the New Testament original text anywhere, and wherever this word does appear in the King James text such as here in Luke, it is simply an unfortunate mistranslation.)

in the New Testament Church Age. Thus, Simeon was filled with the Holy Spirit just as was promised of John, the son of Zacharias in Luke 1:15; and the same as Mary was in fulfillment of what the angel had told her in Luke 1:35; and just like aged Elisabeth was in Luke 1:41. The Holy Spirit was upon him, and in this condition of being filled with the Spirit, the Holy Spirit had revealed to him

> *"that he would not see death before he had seen the Lord's Messiah" (Luke 2:26).*

Our immediate tendency is to assign some special, miraculous character to revelations of this type, but such is not necessarily the case. Remember that it would be 483 years* from the going forth to rebuild the temple, to the coming of the Messiah. Now, it is one of the basic ministries of the Holy Spirit to teach Bible truth from the Word of God to devout men who are positive toward the scriptures. Simeon was such a man. Thus, it was no big deal for the Holy Spirit to reveal to Simeon, as he studied the Word, that it was now very close to 483 years since the rebuilding of the temple, spoken of in Daniel. As a matter of fact, the same kind of revelation was given to Daniel that he might know that the 70 years of their captivity were about completed. This was the basis of their approach to Cyrus, king of Persia, requesting permission to return to Jerusalem to begin the rebuilding of the temple. So really, the only special revelation Simeon received from the Holy Spirit in this regard, was the assurance that he wouldn't see death until he had actually seen the promised Messiah, the Consolation of Israel. Because of this promise, and Simeon's comment in Luke 2:29, we are inclined to ascribe an old age to him, but this too, is not necessarily the case. He was undoubtedly of mature years, but we cannot say that he *"was of a great age,"* as was said of the prophetess Anna, in Luke 2:36.

---

* 62 + 7 weeks or periods of 7 years = 483 years.

So, Simeon knew from his study of the scriptures, as the Holy Spirit taught him, that now was the time for the coming of the Messiah. The 483 years since the rebuilding of the temple were fulfilled, so now was *"the fullness of time"* in this regard also. Thus, Simeon waited and watched expectantly, in faith believing the promises of God, for he was a devout man. And as he waited, we are told in Luke 2:29:

> *"He came at the leading of the Spirit into the temple (on this particular day at this particular hour) when the parents brought in the child Jesus, to do for Him after the custom of the law."*

And when Simeon saw the child, without anyone saying anything, he knew by the same Spirit that this was indeed the Lord's Christ. This is special revelation.

Of all the babies that had been brought into the temple over the months past, I'm sure that Simeon asked himself many times if one of these was the Promised One, but the moment he saw the Baby Jesus, he knew that his faith had been rewarded, for

> *"his eyes indeed had seen the Salvation of Israel"* *(Luke 2:30).*

The statement that Elisabeth made to Mary could also be said of Simeon.

> *"Blessed is (he, Simeon,) that believed: for there shall be a performance of those things which were told (him) of the Lord"* *(Luke 1:45).*

And so it was that Simeon took Jesus up in his arms. As he stood there, not just seeing Him, but actually holding in his own arms the very Son of God, the Messiah of Israel, the Lord's Christ, all he could do was praise and bless his God. This was the highest peak of all the mountain top experiences that Simeon could possibly imagine. Anything else must be anticlimactic. Thus, his statement follows:

> **"Lord, now let thy servant depart in peace according to Thy word: for my eyes have seen (and he could have added, my hands have held) Thy Salvation" (Luke 2:29-30).**

Remember the meaning of the name JESUS? Literally, it means JEHOVAH IS SALVATION. Here was God's Salvation wrapped up in one tiny little Baby. FANTASTIC! Having seen this, what else is there, *"so let thy servant depart."*

This word "depart" was the same word used of the changing of the sentinels in the Roman army at the end of each assigned watch. Simeon had kept his watch faithfully. During that watch, Peace had come in the Person of the Christ Child to earth. So now it was possible for Simeon to depart this earth "in peace." And all of this was in complete fulfillment of the promises of God in His Word.

We don't really know when Simeon died, but we do know he was fully ready to depart, if this was the Lord's will for him. Before he departed from the temple, or the earth, he had just a few more words that the Spirit wanted him to speak regarding "God's Salvation" which he had seen, and was even holding in his arms. This was a Salvation

> **"which God had prepared before the face (or in the presence) of all the peoples" (Luke 2:31).**

This Salvation that Simeon held in his arms was in no way limited to Israel. No, He was

> **"a Light to lighten the Gentiles" (Luke 2:32).**

and for this reason it is possible for us, as Gentiles, to know this Salvation personally. But beyond this, He was *"the Glory of Thy people Israel" (Luke 2:32).*

Of all the things the people of Israel had to glory in throughout their history, nothing compared to this, their ultimate Glory. Yet, nationally, Israel was not to know this Glory as "their Glory" for centuries to come. John tells us in his Gospel:

> *"He came unto His own (His own people) and His own (people) received Him not. But as many as (did) receive Him, to them gave He power (or the right) to become the Sons of God, even to them that believed on His name" (John 1:11- 12).*

And what was that name? JESUS, *"JEHOVAH IS SALVATION."*

Obviously, Joseph and Mary were quite taken aback at all that transpired in this temple experience, and we are told that they

> *"marveled at those things which were spoken of Him" (Luke 2:33).*

One gets the idea that neither Joseph nor Mary really had a grasp of what they were involved in. But, bless God, it isn't always necessary that we understand God's working, in, through, and around us. All He wants of us is our willingness to be used. Marvel if you will, as He goes about His business, but never let that which causes us to marvel, cause us to doubt. THAT is when the marvelous works cease.

Simeon goes on to pronounce a blessing upon the parents and their Baby, and then he makes a statement to Mary in particular. There is not space in this writing to exegete these next two verses, but suffice it to say that, summed up in verses Lk. 2:34-35 is the story of Jesus' experience in His ministry in Israel and the Easter story as well. It serves as a warning to Mary of things to come, so that she might prepare her heart for them. Yet, it seems to leave Joseph out, as though he wouldn't be around to share the experiences Mary was to know. Apparently such was the case, because the last reference we read of Joseph is in Luke 2:48, on the occasion when Jesus' parents lost Him in the temple when He was 12 years old. Sometime in the next 18 years, before Jesus started His earthly ministry, Joseph must have died.

In I John 1:1 & 3, the apostle testifies to the fact that he, like Simeon, had heard, had seen, and his hands had handled the Word of life, the Lord Jesus Christ. But as wonderful a privilege as this was, it is nothing compared to the privilege you and I have. God, in the Person of His Holy Spirit, lives in us, and we are in "living spiritual union" with Christ. We are bone of His bone, and flesh of His flesh (Eph. 5:30). We're not just privileged to see, to hear, or to handle Him, But we are, literally, members of His great Body, the Church (Eph. 1:22-23).

Simeon, we are told, "blessed God" when he saw, and heard, and held the Lord's Christ in his arms. What is our response, then, when we who are united to His Body, bone of His bone, and flesh of His flesh, contemplate all the blessings that are ours in Him? Are we speechless because of our awe and wonder? Or are we speechless because of our ignorance? I pray that we won't be speechless at all, but rather, "bless God" as Simeon did, worshipping and fellowshipping with Him in full participation in everything that that union can provide. I pray that we will be found studying the Word as Simeon did, so that we, too, may be aware of the

"exceeding great and precious promises," (II Peter 1:4)

given to us. These that were given that we may be partakers of that Divine Nature, into which we have been placed, because of our faith in Christ.

Also, in this visit to the temple, they are met by the aged prophetess, Anna, who, in accordance with I Timothy 5:3,5,& 16, is a *"widow indeed,"* and who lived in the temple, giving herself to the ministry of prayer and fasting. If she was married at age 15, which was common, and we are told that she lived with her husband 7 years and then had been a widow 84 years, she would have been at least 106 years old. Yet, she ministered in the temple day and night, in prayers and fasting. Anna truly was an amazing woman.

She also had great praise to the Lord for the privilege of seeing the Messiah, and we are told that she spoke of Jesus to all those who came into the temple, whom she knew to be looking for the coming Messiah, the Redemption of Jerusalem. This tells us that there were numerous devout Jews who frequented the temple who, like Simeon, knew that the 483 years from the rebuilding of the temple were about fulfilled, and thus, they looked expectantly for their Messiah.

Finally, after some time had elapsed (for surely Simeon and Anna's remarks would have created quite a stir among those in the temple), Mary and Joseph were able to get around to the presentation of the Child to the priest, and the offering of the prescribed sacrifices for Mary's purification, that were the reason for their coming to the temple in the first place.

Now we have come to that one verse in this whole account that I believe most commentators overlook in developing the total account surrounding the Christmas story. Luke 2:39 tells us that

"after Mary and Joseph had performed all things according to the law of the Lord, they returned unto Galilee, to their own city Nazareth."

They had left Nazareth approximately 7 weeks before and now they were going back home to Nazareth again, about 65 miles north of Jerusalem in Galilee. This would take them the better part of a week, because they would have to travel slowly for Mary and the Baby to rest often. So from the time they left home until they got back home, approximately 8 weeks has elapsed and the Baby Jesus is about 7 weeks old.

Luke 2:40 & 52 tells us that back in Nazareth,

"The Child grew in all areas of His development. He increased in wisdom, in physical stature, in years and in favor with God and man."

Undoubtedly this covers all the years Jesus spent in Nazareth, both before he was taken down to Egypt and after His return, up until the time He was 12 years old and had the experience related in the remainder of this second chapter of Luke.

Thus we see how the Lord Jesus was born under the law of Moses and was subject to it in every way. In His teaching of the multitude in the sermon on the mount we read in Matthew 5:17, where Jesus said,

"Think not that I am come to destroy the law, or the prophets; I am not come to destroy, but to fulfill."

And so it was that

"God sent forth His Son, made of a woman, made under the law, so that He might redeem them that were under the law, so that we (you and I), might be received, adopted as sons" (Gal. 4:4-5).

Sons of God, even we who believe in His name.

Thus we conclude the study of the Christmas story from Luke's Gospel, but we will see how it is continued in Matthew's gospel in the next chapter.

CHAPTER 6

"There Came Wise Men From the East"

To continue the Biblical account of the total Christmas story, we must now go to Matthew's Gospel where we pick up the new material at Chapter 2. All the events recorded in Chapter 3 through 5 of *The Real Christmas Story* thus far, have taken place since the end of Chapter 1 of Matthew and the beginning of this Chapter 2.

In Matthew 2:1-2 we read:

> *"Now when Jesus was born in Bethlehem of Judaea in the days of Herod the king, behold, there came wise men from the East to Jerusalem, saying, Where is He that is born King of the Jews? For we have seen His star in the East, and are come to worship Him."*

From the wording of the text in the King James, here in Matthew 2:1, it is possible to get the idea that these Wise Men came to Jerusalem at some time during the Holy family's stay in Bethlehem. But, neither the original language, nor the order of events as we have seen them develop thus far from Luke's and Matthew's Gospels, support this contention.

Actually, upward to two years have now elapsed since the birth of Jesus, and He has been back in Nazareth of Galilee for the better part of this time. To establish this fact, I would like to refer you to several other translations

87

of this verse in Matthew 2:1 that is rendered in the King James text:

"Now when Jesus was born in Bethlehem."

The NESTLE GREEK TEXT renders the same phrase thus, *"Now Jesus HAVING BEEN born in Bethlehem..."* (emphasis added) Kenneth Wuest's EXPANDED TRANSLATION OF THE NEW TESTAMENT renders this phrase in exactly the same way. Thus, these translations indicate only that the birth of Jesus in Bethlehem was an event of the past, something that was already an established fact. There is nothing here that would imply that the coming of the Wise Men and the birth of Jesus coincided in any way. The NEW AMERICAN STANDARD BIBLE is even more specific, rendering the phrase, *"Now AFTER JESUS was born in Bethlehem..."* (emphasis supplied). All of these translations, then, would allow almost any length of time between the birth of Christ and the event that our passage is leading up to, that of the coming of the Wise Men to Jerusalem to worship the Christ Child, the One born King of the Jews.

With this thought stored in the back of our minds, let's go back to the account of the coming of the Wise Men, and see just how it develops. Then I believe the picture of just when they came, and where they found the Christ Child will be much clearer.

Our account begins with a statement of the fact that some time after the birth of Jesus in Bethlehem, during the reign of Herod the king, a company of Wise Men from the East came to Jerusalem calling out as they went:

"Where is He that is born King of the Jews? For we have seen His star in the East and are come to worship Him" (Matthew 2:2).

There are several things I would like to point out here. First, there is no generally-held opinion among Bible commentators as to who these wise men really were or where they came from. Also the term "Wise Men" is a much discussed expression, but little is presented in the way of facts about them. They are also called "Magi" which some think carries the idea of their being members of a priestly caste or order of ancient Media and Persia. Others believe them to be the learned class of Magians who cultivated astrology, sorcery and kindred teachings. Still others see them as either Oriental kings or at least king-makers. All we really know from our text is that they were "wise men", their country was east of Jerusalem and that in the original Greek text they are called "magos" or "magian", hence the title "Magi."

These descriptions of the Wise Men seem to depend on all the different definitions one can find for the Greek word "magos" translated "wise" in Matt. 2:1. Strong's Exhaustive Concordance of the Bible identifies them as "a Magian, ie Oriental scientist; by implication a magician:-sorcerer, wise man." As true as all of the above may be, it always seemed to leave me a bit empty in my desire to know who these men actually were. Why were they so interested in the birth of Jesus? What would inspire them to make such a rugged, long and dangerous journey just to spend, at the most, a few hours in His home, where we are told that they fell down and worshipped Him, and presented Him with their gifts? How did they know the star they saw in the east was, indeed, the Christ Child's star? I couldn't believe the Bible would be that silent in this matter.

Since the Bible is primarily a Jewish book, if it did have anything more to say about these men, I surmised that they were probably Jews, and thus, in some way or another descendants of Abraham. As I continued my search I found a clue that broke the whole matter wide open for ME. It had to do with the two captivities, one of Israel and the other of Judah as found in the book of II Kings. Consider the following:

In the ninth year of King Hoshea, the last king of the Northern Kingdom of Israel, the Assyrian army besieged Samaria for three years and finally captured King Hoshea and carried him, along with thousands of others from Israel with him, and made them slaves of the Assyrians. This happened seven hundred forty years before Jesus was born. II Kgs 15:30 and 17:1-6.

Then in 586 B.C., the eighth year that Jehaiakim was king of the Southern Kingdom of Judah, Nebuchadnezzer, king of Babylon carried the king and most of Judah with him and made them slaves of the Babylonians, II Kgs. 24:1, 11-16 and Daniel 1:1. As a result of these two captivities all of the most desirable of the men, women and youths of both the Northern and Southern Kingdoms were ultimately scattered throughout the Babylonian Empire.

Many of these captives were devout Jews who lived in obedience to the Law of Moses. Yet, as is often the case, they were victims of God's judgment on the evil behavior of the leaders of their nation and the multitudes who followed their evil example. In these circumstances, God's Law taught them to be in complete obedience to those in authority over them, even though it be an alien power. Thus, respecting this Law, these captive Jews were so obedient and dependable, and they often showed such wisdom that they began to be trusted with important positions of authority.

For instance, about nine hundred years before these captivities were taken, Joseph, because of his proper attitude and obedience in every circumstance toward his Egyptian masters, rose to be vice-regent over all Egypt under Pharoah. Gen. 39-42.

Also Daniel, who was a youthful captive with those of the Southern Kingdom of Judah, rose to be vice-regent of Babylon under King Nebuchadnezzer by the application of that same doctrine in his life. Both of these men because of their God-honoring attitude, rose to be rulers over the very people who were their captors. Dan. 2:48 tells us, "Then the king (Nebuchadnezzer) made Daniel a great man, and gave him many great gifts, and made him ruler over the whole province of Babylon, and chief of the governors over all the WISE MEN of Babylon." (Emphasis added)

And let us not overlook Shadrach, Meshack and Abednego (Dan. 3), three Hebrew children who were carried into captivity in Babylon with Daniel. Can you imagine any more devout, obedient believers of any age than those captive, courages young men? Their confidence was in their God, regardless of what any man could do to them. I am confident there continued to be many others just like them as long as there were any Jews in Babylon. No, they were not disobedient, they only made an educated, but very difficult and courageous choice and God honored them for it.

Then as we read II Chronicles 36:22-23, and in Ezra 1:1-4 (See pages 13 & 14) under Cyrus, king of Persia, a large contingent of these captive Jews under the leadership of Ezra were allowed to return to rebuild the temple in Jerusalem. Fourteen years after the return of Ezra to Babylon, King Artaxerxes sent a second contingent of captives under the leadership of Nehemiah back to Jerusalem to rebuild the wall and establish civil authority. At no time did even the majority of these captive Jews or their descendants ever return to Israel or Judah. Most of them established new lives in the land of their captors and continued living as best they could, according to God's Law, in obedience to the doctrine of being in subjection to those in authority over them. We have every reason to believe that they also enjoyed the same blessings of God for doing so as was true of Joseph, Daniel and the three Hebrew children.

Thus, it is no problem for me to believe that these devout Jews, especially those who lived after Daniel and his prophecy, were also aware that the 483 year time span between the command by Cyrus to rebuild the temple at Jerusalem unto the birth of the Jews' Messiah spoken of by Daniel in his prophecy, was about to be fulfilled.

Then add to Daniel's prophecy that of Numbers 24:17* and Isaiah 60:3** which they, as students of the Law, would also have known, and it becomes almost obvious why these "Wise Men" were looking for the Christ Child's star at this particular time. Simply stated, these Wise Men were not astrologers, sorcerers, or magicians, they were devout men of God, full of wisdom and the knowledge of God's Word that was available to them at that time. Thus, there were well qualified to be trusted with the truth revealed to them in the Star and what it portended, along with the fantastic experience this truth provided in their journey to Nazareth.

If there is any basis for referring to these travelers as "Wise Men", it is not because of their scientific prowess, but rather that they were filled with the knowledge of God's Word and that they were living in obedience to it. They were looking for the Christ Child's star, and had sense enough to follow it and doggedly seek Him until they found Him. If God could communicate His will to Abram, a moon worshipper of Ur of the Chaldees, He was fully capable of showing these Wise Men that this specific star they had seen was indeed the prophesied star signaling the birth of their Messiah, the Messiah of Israel.

Probably one of the most controversial aspects of the Christmas story is this star which the Wise Men claimed

---

* I shall see him, but not now: I shall behold him, but not nigh: there shall come a Star out of Jacob, and a Sceptre shall rise out of Israel, and shall smite the corners of Moab, and destroy all the children of Sheth. (Numbers 24:17)

** And the Gentiles shall come to thy light, and kings to the brightness of thy rising. (Isaiah 60:3) to have seen in their home country. Just what was it? Was it all some sort of myth, an idea dreamed up by the writer of Matthew's Gospel to add weight to the importance of the birth of Christ? Or, was it some natural phenomenon such as astronomers often see, and for which they generally have a very reasonable explanation? And then, there is the third possibility that it was a special star, every bit as miraculous as the pillar of fire that led the children of Israel at night, or the cloud that led them by day.

Few believe the first possibility, for if this were a figment of the overactive imagination of Matthew, then we couldn't really believe any of his Gospel because we wouldn't know what other portions had a similar character.

As for the natural phenomenon approach, much research has been done. If such an explanation could be established, since most of these occurrences can be dated accurately, it would also, of course, explain the star. So, it was natural for astronomers to try to discern just when these natural phenomena occurred around the approximate time of Christ's birth. Then, because of the uncertainty of the date, as to the actual day and year, these astronomers take the times of these natural phenomena, and try to establish the date when Jesus' birth actually took place.

For instance, there was the conjunction of the planets Jupiter and Saturn in the year 7 B.C. During this year these two planets traveled very close to each other, and in May, September, and December of that year, they were actually conjoined. That is, they were positioned in the heavens so that one star was nearly in line with the other, as seen from earth. Thus, they appeared as one large super-bright star. Then, in February of 6 B.C., the planet Mars joined this conjunction to produce an even larger, and more brilliant light.

93

Of course, the coming together and separating of these stars as they went into and out of conjunction, would then allow for the fact that after the Wise Men had seen the star the first time it apparently disappeared for a while, and then reappeared just as the Wise Men were leaving Herod's court to go to Bethlehem.

Was this the "star" that the Wise Men saw several years before Christ was born that started them on their way to the Holy land? A trip so timed that by the time they arrived in Bethlehem, Jesus' birth was a contemporary event to their arrival? I doubt it very much, because such reasoning leaves too many things to coincidence and speculation. The visit of these Wise Men to Jerusalem, and eventually to the house in which they found the young Child, Jesus, was all a part of the eternal Plan and Program of God. This Plan was established before the foundation of the earth, and I don't believe we need to rely on coincidence or conjecture in this matter of the star. It was too significant a part of the total incarnation experience.

Also, relying on such coincidence and conjecture implies that these Wise Men, these astronomers from the East, couldn't tell the difference between a conjunction and an actual star. Or, it implies that they had some information that was the basis of their belief that this conjunction was the light, the "star" that was to herald His birth. And finally, such reasoning does not fit very well with the simple and explicit statements of scripture.

There were other natural phenomena that occurred in the East at about this time also, such as comets and nova. We are all more or less familiar with comets, but a nova is actually a star that increases many magnitudes in brilliance because of internal explosions that are fantastically spectacular. In most instances these are not visible to the naked eye. These "fire works of nature" also leave much to be desired when we consider the text of Matthew 2:9. Such being the case, we will come back to this subject a little later in this chapter when verse 9 is dealt with.

So, we read in Matthew 2:1-3:

"Behold, there came Wise Men from the East to Jerusalem, calling out as they went along, 'Where is He that is born King of the Jews? for we have seen His own special star in the East and we are come to worship Him.' And when Herod the king had heard these things, he was troubled and all Jerusalem with him." (free translation)

The wording here conveys with it the idea of a very startling experience. The word "Behold" means to "look" or "notice," but in this instance, it is a startled exclamation, LOOK! BEHOLD! Obviously this exclamation, along with the fact that Herod and *"all Jerusalem with him"* were troubled at the presence and the testimony of these men, there had to be more than three of them.

The beloved old Christmas carol begins, "We three kings of Orient are," and this is all that many seem to know about the Wise Men. Yet, it is very doubtful that they were kings and there must have been quite an entourage of them. One tradition sets their number at twelve, while another says there were fourteen. Either of these numbers is probably more accurate than the traditional number of three.

It seems that many assume these Wise Men traveled by camel, yet scripture does not specifically say that they did. It is far more probable that the Wise Men traveled on horses and used camels as their pack animals. Thus, each man would have been riding a horse with at least an equal number of camels to carry the provisions they would have required for such a long journey.

So picture the scene if you can. Twenty or thirty horses and camels with their riders come thundering into Jerusalem calling out:

> *"Where is He that is born King of the Jews? For we have seen His star in the East and are come to worship Him" (Matthew 2:2).*

Their arrival and their questions troubled all Jerusalem, and especially Herod the king. He knew nothing of any King being born, yet there were too many of these men to ignore them. The whole city was upset, and Herod was fit to be tied. So he immediately began an investigation into the matter.

We are told in Matthew 2:4:

> *"And when he (Herod) had gathered all the chief priests and scribes of the people together, he demanded of them where the Christ (the Messiah of Israel) should be born."*

In this verse we begin to learn something about this man King Herod. Whole books have already been written about him and we can't go into great detail here, but it is important that we know just a little about his background, something of his personality, and look at his manner of operation, particularly as these characteristics have to do with this portion of the Christmas Story.

There are several Herods referred to in the Bible, but this is Herod the Great, a title given to him because the Roman Emperor, Augustus, held him in such great respect. He was the son of Herod Antipater who was an Idumean, that is, a descendant of Esau. Thus, on his father's side he was Jewish, but his mother was an Arabian. At the outset of his reign he was a very capable ruler and governed Palestine as a sort of client king in behalf of the Emperor, Caesar Augustus. He reigned a total of 33 years. During this period, he greatly increased the splendor of

Jerusalem, his crowning achievement being the erection of the splendid new Temple there. It was to this temple that the Baby Jesus was brought as recorded in Luke 2:27.

But as Herod's reign continued, his personality and character deteriorated. In his final years a combination of physical illness and court intrigue, combined with growing suspicion and jealousy of everyone around him, he became for all practical purposes, a deranged man. His cruelty was beyond belief. He was so jealous and suspicious of his favorite wife, Mariamne (he had 10 wives), that on two different occasions he ordered that she be killed if he failed to return from an important mission. He finally killed her anyway. He also killed her mother, her grandmother, his own brother-in-law, and three of his own sons as well as many of his subjects. He also ordered the high priest, Aristobulus, to be cunningly drowned. All the while the real trouble maker behind the scene was Herod's sister Salome, who was jealous beyond belief of Herod's wife Mariamne and her sons. She had an uncanny ability to sow seeds of suspicion in Herod's mind and throughout the palace at Jerusalem. As Herod's suspicions and jealousy grew through the lies of his sister (which he was seemingly all too anxious to believe), Herod wrote to Rome time and again for permission to execute another of his sons for treason, until Caesar Augustus made the comment, "I would rather be one of Herod's pigs than one of his sons."

Also, because of the jealousy, suspicion, and intrigue that surrounded not only Herod's palace but also the whole area of Palestine over which he had been made ruler, Herod developed a fantastic intelligence gathering, or G-2 organization. As one commentator put it, "he had a signal corps on every hill top in southern Palestine." It was Herod's army who first put to use the "heliograph," which was an apparatus for telegraphing by means of the sun's rays thrown from a mirror. Actually, his was the first signal corps in history, and the greatest G-2 organization in all the Roman Empire.

From Hebrews 2:14, especially in some of the expanded translations, we see that Jesus, at His birth, took upon Himself flesh and blood, typical of all mankind. But not typical of mankind, He was virgin born, thus, not having an earthly father or an "old sin nature" as all men born of Adam do. So Jesus is the only member of the human race who was **born** outside the devil's kingdom. The devil had no hold on Jesus Christ whatsoever. So, is there any wonder that Satan's one desire was to kill the Baby Jesus? Also, is it any wonder that Herod was the ruler over Palestine at this time? Caesar Augustus may have made Herod's official appointment as ruler over Palestine, but working in the background, directing both Caesar's thoughts and ultimately the thinking of Herod was the prince of this world, Satan himself. And as history records, the nearer it came to the time for the birth of Christ the more Herod behaved like a demon-possessed man.

Yet in spite of all Satan's efforts and the proficiency of Herod's army, God and His forces of righteousness were also working in the background, not in sight, but very much in the fight. He controlled the movements of Joseph and Mary and their little Baby, Jesus. He moved them right through and around the hostile hoards of Satan, and neither these forces, nor Herod's G-2 organization were able to find Him.

As we have already pointed out, there were those in the temple at Jerusalem who knew that the prophecy of 483 years from the order to rebuild the temple until the coming of Israel's Messiah was about to be fulfilled. And we can be sure that if these few faithful men and women looked forward to the Consolation of Israel, Satan was also equally aware that the time for His coming had arrived. And he who didn't stop at trying to usurp the power and authority of the Sovereign God of the universe, would also not hesitate to destroy the Son of God, now incarnate in this body of flesh and blood.

Having laid this background, we now come back to our passage in Matthew 2:4, where we read that this "mad man of the *Christmas story*," Herod, had

> *"called all the chief priests and the scribes of the people (the Jews) together."*

No one who might contribute information in any way was left out. And then we read:

> *"he demanded of them (not asked, but demanded) where the Christ (their Messiah) should be born."*

And they had a ready answer. In verses 5 and 6 we read:

> *"And they (the chief priests and scribes) said unto him, '(He shall be born) in Bethlehem of Judaea, for this is the way His coming is recorded in the prophets."*

And then they go on to read or quote to Herod the prophecy from Micah 5:2. Now this prophecy was given over 700 years before this event took place and yet they had that specific promise of God as a ready reference when asked a reason for this hope of Israel (compare I Peter 3:15). All down through the history of Israel the promise of a Messiah Redeemer had been the key to their faith in first one trial of testing after another until finally, Daniel tells them specifically, "it will be 483 years from now."

It is in light of this specific information that I find it incredible that so few, especially among the learned of Israel, the chief priests and scribes of the temple who were given the responsibility for the keeping of this information, so few, believed that the time was indeed at hand. as did Simeon, Anna and others who looked for the

Consolation of Israel. Here again, we see revealed the mortal deadness of spirituality in Israel in that day.

This information was given by the Holy Spirit of God to His prophets as Micah 5:2 records:

"But thou, Bethlehem Ephratah, though thou be little (approximately 180 people at the time Micah wrote) among the thousands of Judah, yet out of thee shall He come forth unto Me that is to be Ruler in Israel; Whose goings forth (Whose origins) have been from of old, from everlasting."

Thus, since this prophecy was given of God, it follows that the fulfillment of this prophecy would also be under the government of God. So everything that had transpired throughout this total Christmas story has been under the ultimate control and supervision of God. Beginning with Zacharias and Elisabeth, the choice of Mary, of Joseph, the decree of Caesar Augustus, Bethlehem, the no-room-at-the-inn situation, the manger, the shepherds, the angels, the host of angelic beings, Simeon, Anna, the star, the Wise Men and now Herod, all have been no more than pawns on a great eternal chess board and God is the only player.

Now Herod knows where Jesus was to be born. But remember, neither he, nor apparently any of the chief priests or scribes realize that His birth had actually taken place several months before the coming of these Wise Men. The background of the account of Jesus' birth that you and I have up to this point was not available to Herod or his advisers. All they knew was He was to be born in Bethlehem.

Thus, after getting this information from the chief priests and scribes, Herod sends these informants away. And, when they were well out of sight, Matthew 2:7 tells us, that

> *"Herod secretly called the Wise Men in to the palace and inquired of them very carefully what time the star appeared."(free translation)*

That is, he made sure he knew just exactly how long it had been since the star had made itself visible in its rising in the east. You can be sure that when Herod was finally finished interrogating these Wise Men, always under the guise of wanting also to worship the new born King, there wasn't much that they knew that he didn't also know. He knew when and where they first saw the star. He undoubtedly knew something about the reason for their visit, how they had come, and how long it took them to get there. Then, when he was satisfied that he had all the information they had to give him, he told them what he knew. Jesus was to be born in Bethlehem of Judah, five or six miles down the road. And where did he get his information? From a 700 year old prophecy from the prophets of Israel. That is all he knew to give them.

And so we are told, in Matthew 2:8, that

> *"He sent them to Bethlehem, and said; Go and search diligently for the young Child(not an infant any longer on the basis of the information he has just received) and when you have found him, bring me word that I may come and worship Him also."*

From the information they gave Herod, Jesus is always referred to as a *"young child"* hereafter in Matthew 2.

It is in the intrigue and secrecy with which everything is done here that we see the real motive behind Herod's instruction to the Wise Men. Why did he meet with them in secret? Why didn't he want the chief priests or the scribes to hear their story? Why didn't he send the chief priests or the scribes who, one would think would have been much more qualified to identify their own Messiah than these foreigners would have been? The last thing

101

Herod wanted was for these Israelites to find their Messiah. They were hard enough to control as they were, and this new Babe just might represent a rallying point for them. Herod surely didn't need that on top of all his other problems. It would be easier just to find out where the Child was, have Him killed, and most of Palestine would be none the wiser. Then he let these Wise Men, who are also none the wiser for what they learned from him, help him with his dirty work. And thus, he sent them on their way.

And as they left Herod's palace, undoubtedly headed six miles down the road to Bethlehem, we are told with some exclamation:

> *"and BEHOLD! the star which they had seen in the east went before them, until it came and stood over where the young child (not an infant) was" (Matthew 2:9).*

The very same star, the one that they had seen back in their own country, and which had apparently not been visible for some time now, reappeared right at this moment of their departure from Herod's palace, to now guide them in this final stage of their journey right to where the young Child was.

It is here that I part company with the majority of commentators who deal with this visitation of the Magi to the house where Jesus is now living. Keep in mind that Luke tells us in 2:39 that after Jesus' parents had performed everything in the temple in the way of sacrifices that were required for both Mary and the Baby, *"they returned into Galilee, to their own city Nazareth."* And we know that this would have been on the fortieth day after Jesus was born, according to Luke 2:22 and Leviticus 12:2-4. So now, to get the events of this story straight, we must get the timing straight. When this is accomplished everything falls neatly into place.

First of all, regardless of how reluctant mankind is to accept the supernatural, I don't believe it is necessary to intelligent understanding, and exegesis of the Word, to eliminate it all together from this account. Therefore, I do not believe that the star these Wise Men saw in their home country was a natural phenomenon any more than the pillar of fire by night or the cloud by day that led the Children of Israel through the wilderness were natural phenomena. The main reason for my position is the fact stated here in Matthew 2:9. The very same star that these Wise Men had seen in the East now reappeared and "went before them," just like the pillar of fire guided the Israelites on their wilderness journey. *"It went before them until it came and stood over where the young child was."* According to Matthew 2:11, the young Child was in a house. Then, according to Luke 2:39, this house was in Nazareth of Galilee, 65 miles to the north, and not in Bethlehem. So the star led them step by step to where the young Child was. Now, I contend that natural phenomenon type of stars do not go before to lead men six miles down the road. There was something supernatural about this star just like there was something supernatural about every other aspect of this virgin birth.

So it is not unreasonable, in the light of other teachings in the Bible, to accept the premise that the Sovereign God of the universe attracted the attention of these Magi in their own country by means of this special supernatural light that they called a star. Then, after getting their attention in this way, God revealed to them what this star was all about, using the same method He employed to show that moon worshiper, Abram (Genesis 12:1), that He wanted him to move out of Ur of the Chaldees (Genesis 11:31) and go to a land that God would show him. Remember, Abram packed bag and baggage. He took his entire family, his slaves, his cattle, everything he had, and started walking, and as Hebrews 11:8 tells us, *"he didn't know where he was going."* It seems God had a way of

103

getting people to move in those days that isn't available in the Church today.

So I am willing to believe that God revealed to the Wise Men, in a way, the knowledge of which He has reserved for Himself, even as He revealed to the shepherds, as we have already been shown, that the Messiah, the King of the Jews was born. God didn't tell the Wise Men, at the time they first saw the star in the east, that Jesus was born in the city of David, because He knew that by the time they arrived there, Jesus would be living in Nazareth of Galilee. So instead, God reserved for these Magi a miraculous second appearance of their special star.

Going back to the timing factor, I trust by now that you are as convinced as I am that these Wise Men were devout Jews from somewhere in the Babylonian Empire, at this time under Roman rule. Such being the case, it would have taken them something like the four months that Ezra required to travel from Babylon to Jerusalem as we are shown in Ezra 7:9, once they got under way. They would also have to prepare for such a long trip and additional time would be required for this preperation.

To narrow down this timing element, we go back to Herod. In reading the full text from Matthew we see that six times in the seven verses of Matt. 2:8- 14, Jesus is referred to as a "young child." Then, in Matt. 2:16 we read that this mad man, Herod, "slew all the young children from two years old and under." Why two years? This timing was based on what Herod had learned when he so carefully inquired of these Wise Men, as to when they had seen the Lord's star in the east. Also, I don't believe that any long period of time elapsed between the time the Wise Men left Herod's palace until he began to suspect that he had been mocked (Matt. 2:16); because, as we have already pointed out, Bethlehem was just a few miles away, and it would not be long before he would have been expecting them back.

We know then that some time shortly after these Magi appeared in Herod's court, he began his brutal and heartless massacre of the male children in and around Bethlehem,

"who were two years old and under, according to the time which he had so carefully inquired of the Wise Men" (Matt 2:16).

From this, then, we can reasonably assume that Jesus was approximately two years old when the Wise Men found Him, and that this was the time required for them to prepare for and make their journey. They found Him in a house in Nazareth of Galilee, because this is where the miraculous star led them. How glad they were for this star, which not only started them on this journey, but also guided them step by step the last few miles of their way.

Matt 2:10 tells us that

"when they saw the star, they rejoiced with exceeding great joy."

Now they knew the purpose of their journey was about to be realized. And when the star stopped, it stopped right over the house where Jesus was. And then, we are told in Matt. 2:11 that

"when they were come into the house, they saw the young child Jesus, with His mother Mary, and they fell down and worshipped Him."

Not His mother, not Him and His mother.

"They ... worshipped Him."

Then, as a part of this worship and homage that they paid to the Lord Jesus Christ they also opened their treasure chests, and from them presented gifts to Jesus consisting of gold, frankincense and myrrh. It was the custom in those days, even as it is today, for gifts to be presented to kings and heads of state when foreign dignitaries came to pay them a visit. For instance, when Solomon became king in Israel, Hiram, his father David's friend, sent him over 12 million dollars worth of gold, precious stones, and spices (I Kings 10:10). So, the gifts that these Wise Men brought to Jesus were typical of the gifts that foreign dignitaries would bring, especially when they were visiting a new king that they held in the great esteem that these Wise Men obviously felt for this One born King of the Jews.

We must also ask the question, was there any significance to the types of gifts listed here? Gold was always included, because it recognized the kingly position, the royalty of the one being honored. There was a practical aspect about this also since God knew that before many days passed, Joseph and Mary were going to need ready cash for their quick departure, and for their stay in Egypt. So what better gift than gold which could be universally exchanged in any country for the coin of that realm?

But what is frankincense and myrrh? Why would these men bring these spices to this new born King. As we have already pointed out, the Queen of Sheba brought a great abundance of spices, more that anyone else, to king Solomon, and I am sure these spices of frankincense and myrrh would have been among her great treasure. But here the gift of spices these Wise Men brought to Jesus is peculiar in its limitation. Apparently these were the only spices they brought to Him. As a gift, the gold was very appropriate, acknowledging our Saviour's Kingly position, His Royalty. But viewed as gifts, the frankincense and myrrh would, indeed, have been strangely inappropriate. Thus, they are all the more significant.

Once again I have to reflect on what we who have the Bible for study and comparison know of types and symbols in the Old Testament, and what people like these

Wise Men may have known. We are often prone to ascribe more knowledge and intent to them than they could possibly have manifested. Such being the case, it was highly probable that the gold brought by the Wise Men to Jesus was the only true gift they brought, while the frankincense and myrrh were merely products of their home country that they brought as a means of expressing the homage of that country to the new-found King. This practice is common today throughout the world. Also since the production of frankincense was common to southern Arabia, Babylon and India, this fact is of no help in pinpointing the origin of these Wise Men either.

But again, behind every action and phenomenon of this Christmas Story must be seen the Will and Plan of the Sovereign God of the universe. And He is fully capable of taking the every day ordinary actions of His creatures, and turning them into significant signs and symbols relating to aspects of His Divine Plan. So it was with the frankincense and myrrh these Wise Men brought.

Frankincense is a white gum-like resin, taken from the incense tree, and usually consisting of small beads or pieces, that were then ground into powder. In this form it was used extensively in the different sacrifices of the temple. When it was burned it gave off a fragrant aroma much like balsam. It was also used in perfumes, and for fumigation, during the burning of the offerings.

Myrrh was also a gum resin taken from a small shrub or bush that grew in Yemen, and in neighboring regions of Africa. It was bitter to the taste, and was sometimes used as a drug to relieve pain. Its color ranged from a pale orange to reddish brown to red, and it was very expensive. It was much sought after in fine perfumes, and was used for embalming in fine funerals.

It can be seen that so far as practical value was concerned, neither of these spices represents much worth to this small Baby, or the parents. It might have been sold,

107

but what kind of gift is it that has to be sold to realize its practical worth? Thus its symbolic meaning becomes all the more important even though these Magi may not have realized it.

So it is that most commentators agree that in their symbolism, these gifts carry their greatest significance. The gold, while having the greatest immediate practical value, actually recognized Jesus' Royalty. Frankincense symbolizes Jesus' Deity. It points to the fact that He was indeed the very Son of God, sent to earth to be the

"Lamb of God that taketh away the sins of the world" (John 1:29).

It also looks forward to Christ's spiritual death on the cross. Finally, myrrh, called "symrna" in the Greek, looks forward to Christ's physical death on the cross. It symbolizes His physical suffering on our behalf.

And so it was that these Wise Men presented their gifts and homage to their new-found King. No evidence is given that they spent more than a relatively brief time in the house where Jesus lived during their visit. Yet we are shown that they received a warning in a dream from God that they should not report back to Herod as he had instructed them. Obviously then, God was directing these men just as surely as he was Mary, Joseph, the shepherds, Simeon, Anna and all the rest of the primary characters in this Christmas Story. God had spoken to them to start them on their journey, and He would continue instructing them until they had returned home safely. We are told also that God spoke to them in a dream, just as He had done, and would do two more times to Joseph.

Now if these men had visited Jesus in Bethlehem as so many commentators imply, when would they have had opportunity for God to have warned them in a dream? They would have made their trip to this small city of David, paid their homage, left their gifts, and returned to

Jerusalem in less than a day. But if they had gone to Nazareth of Galilee, as I believe the scriptures teach, then they would have stopped to rest for the night several times in the few days it would have taken them to make the 65 mile trip. Thus, before they ever arrived at the home in Nazareth they already had their instructions about not reporting back to Herod. Such being the case they returned to their own country by a different route, one that took them away from Jerusalem, probably straight east or even north of the Sea of Galilee and then east, just the opposite route that Abram ultimately took to get to Canaan.

Thus the Magi exit from the Christmas Story, but the effect of their having been a part of it would be felt for some time to come.

CHAPTER 7

"Out of Egypt Have I Called My Son"
(Matt. 2:15).

The Wise Men or Magi have now gone back to their own country, but their coming has revealed to Herod (the "mad man" of this Christmas story), that Jesus has indeed been born. Further, it was also revealed from heaven that this Baby is ultimately to reign as King of the Jews, and this was more than the suspicious, evil mind of this puppet-king could stand.

But, God in His omniscience knew all that was in Herod's mind. When Herod sent the Wise Men to find Jesus, telling them that he wanted to go worship Him also, God knew that this wasn't what Herod had in mind at all. So He warned the Wise Men in a dream to get out of the country, and not go back to see Herod. God also knew what Herod's attitude would be when he learned that these Wise Men had mocked or snubbed him, and had left the country without telling him what he wanted to know. So God also warned Joseph in a dream that he should

> *"take the young Child and His mother, and flee into Egypt, and be thou there until I bring thee word: for Herod will seek the young Child to destroy Him" (Matt. 2:13).*

111

It has been a matter of much speculation why a man of Herod's age would be so concerned over an infant child, who, if he were to succeed him, couldn't possibly do so for fifteen or twenty years. And, Herod was already nearly 70 years old. He couldn't hope to live until **this** young Child became a threat to his throne. And, of course, history bears this out for Herod died in his seventieth year.

All of this is a demonstration of how deranged his mind had become. It was as though he was wholly given over to evil and violence. So it was natural for him in his later years to react in this way, thinking to seek out and destroy anyone, regardless of who they were, who might represent a threat in any way to his rulership.

Thus it was that God warned Joseph in a dream. Some have called it a nightmare, in which he was instructed to flee with the young Child and His mother to Egypt for protection. So, when Joseph awoke from his sleep, we are told that he was obedient to this divinely given instruction as he had been two and a half years earlier, when, by the same means, God had revealed to him that the Baby tabernacled in Mary's womb was indeed of the Holy Spirit. At that time, he took Mary to be his wife. Now, when he arises from his sleep, he immediately takes Mary and the young Child and flees in the middle of the night into Egypt. So the Wise Men left Nazareth of Galilee by one route, and Joseph, Mary and the Child left Nazareth of Galilee by another. Herod, in spite of his highly developed and efficient G-2 system, was none the wiser until it was too late. In spite of his highly developed use of the heliograph, there was no sun to make it work. God is never at a loss to look after those who are busy doing what he has instructed. And the *"hosts of heaven"* were still around, even as they were throughout Jesus' life, protecting Him from all harm until the time appointed for His death should come.

But on top of this, it is obvious from Matt. 2:16 that Herod was not aware that Jesus was now in Nazareth of Galilee instead of Bethlehem. All he knows at this time is that this is where the chief priests and the scribes told him their Messiah King was to be born. The intervening events that we have studied between the birth of Jesus and this flight into Egypt could not have been made known unto him. And this fact, of course, made Joseph's flight into Egypt with his little family, all the more sure of success. It would be real comforting when you are being hunted by a mad man such as Herod, who wants to destroy you, to have him looking in the wrong place while you are fleeing to safety.

Also, we are not told why Herod, with his great intelligence corps, never had these Wise Men followed to make sure that nothing happened, to prevent his learning of the Child's whereabouts. I am convinced that he didn't want anyone but himself to know where Jesus was so that his planned destruction of the Christ Child could be accomplished with as little fuss as possible. Thus, he had to trust the naivete of the Wise Men to fulfill their mission and return as he had instructed. But he hadn't calculated on God's ability to communicate His will to these Wise Men, or to Joseph. Herod is left to his own devices. True to his nature, and in great wrath at being snubbed by the Wise Men, he worked out another of his fiendish plans of murder and mayhem.

Since Jesus was to be born in Bethlehem as the prophecy of Micah foretold, and since Herod had no information that would lead him to believe He was living anywhere else, Herod ordered his troops to slay all the children in and around Bethlehem who were up to two years old. This age limit was established because it agreed with the information he had gotten from the Wise Men when Herod so carefully interrogated them in his palace.

113

We are not told how many children were slain in this carnage, but since Bethlehem was still one of the rather small communities of Judah, the number of children in this two year age group could have been fewer than twenty. I mention this, not to make Herod's crime any the less terrible, but to help us get a picture of the reality of the event. Twenty infants slain should indeed stimulate the wrath and ire of all the just and decent of mankind, but there was very little justice or decency in Israel or anywhere else in the Roman Empire of that day, and Herod was a past master in the act of assassination and murder.

Herod had just taken over the throne in Jerusalem when he began to annihilate, one by one, the Sanhedrin. This was the supreme court of the Jews. Later, in an almost off-hand manner, he slaughtered three hundred officers of his court. After this he had his wife Mariamne murdered. Then, he murdered her mother, Alexandra. He executed Mariamne's eldest son named Antipater, and two of his other sons, Alexander and Aristobolus. He also had Mariamne's grandfather and her brother murdered along with another of his brothers-in-law, who was also the high priest.

Then, as Herod got older, and suffering from hardening of the arteries, he began to fear that no one would mourn his death. A safe assumption indeed. So he devised another mad scheme to insure there would be mourning in Israel when he died. He called all the principal men from all over the Jewish nation to his bedside. And, although the record is not detailed, it is said that a great number came. Then, after railing at them from his death bed, he had the whole lot of them locked into the great Hippodrome at Jericho, and gave instructions from his death bed that when he finally died, the soldiers should shoot all these men with arrows, until they were dead. Thus, the mourning in Israel would be, as he said, "from the soul rather than in sport and mockery."

I present this information about these other hideous crimes of Herod to show that he was in no way above slaying a few babies in Bethlehem if this was the only way he could be sure that *"He who was born King of the Jews"* would be permanently eliminated.

These were the last two orders given by Herod involving assassination and murder. The first, the destruction of the babies at Bethlehem so that he could destroy the Jews' Messiah King; the second, the order to destroy the great company of the leaders of the Jewish Nation, to intensify the mourning in Israel at his death. yet neither order accomplished its intended purpose. Though the babies were slain at Bethlehem, Jesus was not among them. He and His family were safely waiting out the news of Herod's own death somewhere in Egypt!

And not long after Joseph and his family fled to Egypt, Herod died from an extremely painful and loathsome disease. The historian Josephus tells us that after attempting suicide and failing at this also, Herod finally contracted a very loathsome disease, early in 4 B.C., which ulcerated his digestive system, inflamed his abdomen, rotted his privates to the extent that it produced worms. So loathsome was his condition that when he was raised to a sitting position, the stench so offended him that it blocked his breathing. He finally died in a great fever, and with convulsions that racked his entire body.

But the principal men of the Jewish nation who were shut up in the Hippodrome were not slain as Herod had ordered. Instead, they were actually released before Herod's death was made known and were sent back to their own lands.

A bit of background is necessary here to help us understand Joseph's decision as described in Matt. 2:22. At Herod's death, his will, which he changed three different times in the last year of his life, divided his kingdom between three of his sons.

115

To Archelaus he willed at least half of his kingdom which included Judea, Idumea and Samaria (Jerusalem and Bethlehem were in this area). This was the wealthier half of Herod's kingdom and it yielded twice as much revenue as the other half. Herod also assigned the title of "king" to Archelaus and he was saluted as such after his father's death. Archelaus began his reign as his father had ended his, in murder and mayhem. He massacred three thousand Jews who had rebelled against him in the temple at Jerusalem. So in Judea, human life was still cheap and blood flowed freely.

Another son, Herod Antipas, was made Tetrarch of Galilee and Pera where Nazareth was located. The Greek word "tetrarch" originally signified the ruler of a fourth part of a province or district. But, it was later applied by the Romans in the time of our Lord, to the ruler over any considerable part of a province of people. Herod Antipas is the ruler who appears in connection with John the Baptist, and in the public ministry of our Lord.

A third portion of Herod's kingdom was given to his son Herod Philip, who was made Tetrarch of Iturea and Trachonitis, as well as some adjacent districts. This is the Philip mentioned only in Luke 3:1.

So Joseph and his little family find themselves in hiding in Egypt, awaiting word, as the angel had told him in his dream, that it was safe to return to his home land. We are told nothing about where they spent their sojourn in Egypt, or what Joseph may have done to support his family while they were there. Several large communities of Jews had been permanently established in Egypt under Alexander the Great, the more prominent of which was at Alexandria. It is doubtful that Joseph would have traveled this far into Egypt, but he would have been made welcome in any one of these Jewish settlements. Also, he could have plied his trade as a carpenter to earn support for his family.

It is generally agreed that they did not spend more than a few months in Egypt, for it was not long after the killing of the children in and around Bethlehem that Herod died. It would have taken several weeks of this time for them to travel into Egypt. Thus, Joseph and Mary would hardly have had time to put down any permanent roots in Egypt, before the Angel spoke to Joseph for the third time in a dream:

"Saying, Arise, and take the young Child and His mother, and go into the Land of Israel: for they are dead which sought the young Child's life" (Matt. 2:19-20).

And, as has been Joseph's habit on each occasion of these heavenly nocturnal instructions, immediately

"He arose and took the young Child and His mother and came into the land of Israel" (Matt. 2:21).

As Joseph, Mary, and the young Child traveled back into Israel, they would have entered first into the area of Idumea, which was still remote from Jerusalem, but a part of Herod's kingdom, willed to his son Archelaus. It is not likely that Joseph could have been aware of the events that had transpired in Israel since he had left at the instruction of the angel, so quickly and quietly in the middle of the night, a few months earlier. Thus, the angel had to inform him that Herod was dead to start them on their way home. As Joseph entered Idumea with his family, it was only natural that he try to catch up on the news of his homeland as soon as possible. So it was that he learned that Herod's son, Archelaus was ruling in Judea in place of his father, and with this news, undoubtedly came the information relative to the slaughter of the three thousand Jews in the temple, when Archelaus took over the reign of his father. He also would have learned at this time that Herod Antipas was ruler in Galilee, and his brother Herod Philip ruled over Iturea and Trachonitis.

From an economic standpoint Joseph could probably earn the best living at his trade as a carpenter in the area of Jerusalem and Bethlehem, since this was the wealthiest part of the entire nation of Israel. But, being a good father, and the devout Jew that he was, it was natural that he would be reluctant, even fearful, of taking his family into such a situation as Judea represented under the tyrannical reign of Archelaus. This was especially true in light of the attitude Archelaus had shown already to the Jews.

Thus it was that as he thought on just what he should do, once again God made His Will known to Joseph as he slept on the matter. God warned him again in a dream of the hazards that threatened the Christ Child in the area of Judea. So Joseph promptly turned aside from settling his family in Judea and traveled on north, most likely following the coastal route along the western edge of Judea, well away from Jerusalem and Bethlehem, until they arrived once again at Nazareth, out of the jurisdiction of Archelaus.

> **But when he heard that Archelaus did reign in Judaea in the room of his father Herod, he was afraid to go thither: notwithstanding, being warned of God in a dream, he turned aside into the parts of Galilee: And he came and dwelt in a city called Nazareth: that it might be fulfilled which was spoken by the prophets, He shall be called a Nazarene (Matthew 2:22-23).**

Once again they were back home. Back to the poor little village of Nazareth of Galilee, concerning which, Nathanael had asked Philip (John 1:45), *"Can there any good thing come out of Nazareth?"* Back to the place where it all began when Mary and Joseph were espoused to be married. Back where the angel Gabriel had first greeted

Mary, and where Mary had so fully and completely committed herself, body, soul and spirit unto God for His use. And God did, indeed, use her. What a fantastic experience it had been, but through it all, God had His hand upon them at all times. The road was exceedingly rough at times but God was leading. There were mountain top experiences, too, but they invariably led to *"the valley of the shadow of death."* Yet God walked this valley with them.

Surely,

"Faithful is He that calleth you, who also will do it" (I Thessalonians 5:24).

"God is faithful, by Whom ye were called" (I Corinthians 1:9).

And as the Christmas Story is completed, we have looked at the account from both Luke and Matthew. There are many things that could have been elaborated on, such as the prophecies that were mentioned in Matthew's account that were fulfilled: (1) when the young Child was taken into Egypt (Matt. 2:13), (2) when Herod slew the young children around Bethlehem (Matt. 2:17-18), and (3) when they finally settled in Nazareth, that Jesus might be called a Nazarene. These are all important matters, but since Jesus in the incarnation fulfilled so many prophecies, and this is not a study of prophecy, I elected to pass over them. Also, the discourse of Mary in Luke 1:46-55 is worthy of a book by itself. Never a teen-aged girl before or since has preached such a sermon as Mary delivered in these verses.

I suppose the one word that is pre-eminent throughout this discourse on the events surrounding the birth of Christ, is the word "obedience." Obedience that manifested explicit faith and confidence in the One obeyed.

119

Mary believed the angel Gabriel and trusted his message completely. Because she did, there was a performance of all that the angel had promised (Luke 1:45). She was obedient to his word, and her obedience was rewarded by fantastic Fruit of the Spirit.

Joseph likewise manifested obedience at every turn, and God rewarded his faith in a similar manner. It is striking to me how God elected to speak to Joseph always while he slept. Four different times, God's message and will was revealed to Joseph, and each time it was in a dream (Matt. 1:20, 2:13). Each time his response was immediate obedience. This attitude of prompt obedience on the part of Joseph tells me much about him, though it is sketchy at best. Joseph always desired, it seems, to know the will of God for himself and for this young Child. He was ever obedient to what this will dictated. For this reason, God was always sure that Joseph understood His will whenever there was something He wanted Joseph to do. He is a personification of John 7:17 where we read:

"If any man is willing to do His will, he shall know of the teaching." (NASB)

Joseph, too, believed God, as Mary did. Because of this, he is said to be a *"just man,"* one "justified" in the eyes of God.

We are back now to that place in the life of Christ between verses 39 and 40 of Luke 2. Verses 40 through 52 tell only a little of the life of Christ before he begins His public ministry at age 30 (Luke 3:23). Thus, our look at the portion of scripture known as the Christmas Story is concluded. At this point, one should go on to a study of the Life of Christ. If you have never entered into such a study, I commend it to you as a life changing experience.

CHAPTER 8

Was Jesus Born on December 25?

Although the actual day of Jesus' birth has been lost to history, and thus has never been considered an integral part of the Christmas Story, the time of the year can be ascertained reasonably close from Scripture, and by comparing the pertinent Hebrew calendar months with their corresponding months on our regular Roman or Gregorian calendar. But before we look at these calendars let us establish some facts from Scripture.

In the first chapter of Luke's Gospel we have recorded the account of the ministry of the faithful priest Zacharias in the temple, and how the angel appeared unto him, bringing the promise that a son would be born to this aged couple, and that he should name the child, John. Also pointed out in this chapter in careful detail is the order of events that lead up to the conception of Zacharias' wife Elisabeth. Further in Luke 1, we have described the conception of Mary by the Holy Spirit, and the timing of this event in relation to Elisabeth's conception. That is, Mary conceived six months after Elisabeth.

And in the sixth month the angel Gabriel was sent from God unto a city of Galilee, named Nazareth, (Luke 1:26)

And, behold, thy cousin Elisabeth, she hath also conceived a son in her old age: and this is the sixth

121

month with her, who was called barren (Luke 1:36).

This six months time span is further verified in Luke 1:56-57, where we are told that Mary spent three months with Elisabeth immediately after Mary's conception.

"And Mary abode with her about three months, and returned to her own house. Now Elisabeth's full time came that she should be delivered; and she brought forth a son" (Luke 1:56-57).

Then, at the end of this three months' visit, Elisabeth's full nine months time was complete, and she delivered the promised son, John. Thus, if we can establish when John was born, we know that Jesus was born six months later.

To establish the time of John's birth it is necessary to present a little background on the activities of the priests in the temple, to see just how Zacharias would have been functioning in his ministry at the time the angel of Luke 1:11 appeared to him. To do this, let's begin by noting Exodus 30:1-10, particularly verses 6 through 8.

In the first five verses of Exodus 30, God is describing to Moses how the altar of incense is to be constructed for use in the tabernacle. Then, in verses 6-8, He tells Moses where this altar is to be located in the Holy Place of the tabernacle, and how the priests are to minister at this altar.

"And thou shalt put it (the altar of incense) before the veil that is by the ark of the testimony, before the mercy seat that is over the testimony, where I will meet with thee. And Aaron shall burn thereon sweet incense every morning: when he dresseth the lamps (the golden lamp stand) he shall burn incense upon it. And when Aaron lighteth the lamps at even, he shall burn incense

upon it, a perpetual incense before the Lord throughout your generations" (Ex. 30:6-8).

We see from these verses that there were specific duties for the priest to perform each morning and evening as part of their ministry in the tabernacle.

Now, notice some further instructions about the way the priests should go about preparing themselves for their ministry in the tabernacle, when it was their turn to serve in this capacity.

"And ye shall not go out of the door of the tabernacle of the congregation in seven days, until the days of your consecration be at an end: for seven days shall he consecrate you" (Lev. 8:33-35).

From this verse we learn that the first seven days of the priest's ministry in the tabernacle was spent in preparing themselves for the ministry, and then they actually ministered after that. At no time in this period of preparation or ministry did the priests leave the tabernacle.

Then, in I Chronicles, chapters 24, 25, 26 and 27, we read of the appointment of all those who were to minister in any way to Israel. These are four very important chapters. The appointments were made not only for the purpose of knowing who would minister for Israel in each year, but they also established the length and order of their ministry each year.

Thus we see in I Chr. 24 how the sons of Aaron were divided into 24 lots or orders, to occupy the office of Priest consecutively each year, a half month at a time. Chapter 26 tells of the appointment of the porters to tend the gates, the Levites to be in charge of the treasuries, and the officers and judges to rule over the people. Then, in chapter 27, we have the account of the appointment of the 12 captains, each over 24,000 men. These captains were to serve consecutively, each serving for one month of the year. Everything was set in a very definite order. Each group and each person knew exactly what they were assigned to do, they knew how they were to prepare for this service, and they knew precisely when they were to minister in their service.

We would do well to study each of these four chapters carefully, but it is chapter 24 that we are concerned with now, since it is this chapter that tells us about the ministry of Zacharias, the father of John the Baptist. It enables us to determine the time of the conception and birth of John, and consequently that of Jesus, since Jesus was six months younger than John.

At the end of this book there is a chart showing the time of Zacharias' ministry in the Temple, the time of Elisabeth's conception, the time of Mary's conception, the time of John's birth, and the time of Jesus' birth. It will be obvious that by "time," we do not mean the exact day or hour, but only the month. From here on you will find it helpful to refer to this chart a number of times as you read.

A comparison of Deut. 16:1, Lev. 23:5 and Ex. 12:2 will show that the first month of the year was "Abib"; in the nation of Israel. A comparison of a Hebrew and Roman calendar will show that this month "Abib" corresponds with the last nine days of March, and the first twenty one days of April. Essentially Abib is April (see the chart).

Zacharias is said to be a priest of the order of Abia (Greek) or Abijah (Hebrew) as noted in Luke 1:5

"There was in the days of Herod, the king of Judaea, a certain priest named Zacharias, of the course of Abia: and his wife was of the daughters of Aaron, and her name was Elisabeth."

This order (course) is named in the 24 courses in I Chr. 24:10 as the eighth course, and would minister in the Temple during the last half of the fourth month, which is Thammuz on Israel's calendar, or the middle of our month of July (see the chart).

Zacharias and his wife are said to be

"walking in all the commandments and ordinances of the Lord, blameless" (Luke 1:6).

This tells us that even though most of the other priests of that day were corrupted, Zacharias was not so. He was faithful in every respect, fully obeying God's Word to the letter. But they were childless and well stricken in years.

We read that Zacharias was executing the priest's office in the "order" of his course:

"And it came to pass, that while he executed the priest's office before God in the order of his course" (Luke 1:8).

This means that he was occupying this office during the time assigned to Abia or Abijah, which was the middle of our month of July (see the chart).

In the intervening verses we have the account of Zacharias ministering, by burning incense at the Golden Altar of Incense as the multitude of the people prayed outside. And as he ministered at the altar of incense, Gabriel, the angel of the Lord appeared at the right side of the altar and Zacharias was terror stricken. But the angel acknowledges him and quiets his fear, telling him that his prayer for a son has been heard. Thus Elisabeth, in spite of her great age, would conceive and bear a son and Zacharias would name him John.

The angel Gabriel goes on to tell him all about this child, and of some of the unusual things that would be true of their son. And the angel confirmed this promise with a sign, the sign of Zacharias' deafness and dumbness.

So it was, we read:

"And it came to pass, that AS SOON AS the days of his ministration were accomplished, he departed to his own house. And AFTER THOSE DAYS his wife Elisabeth conceived..." (emphasis supplied)(Luke 1:23-24).

This is important. *"AS SOON AS"* leaves no interval at all. Zacharias went home to Elisabeth immediately following his 15 days of ministry in the temple. *"And AFTER THOSE DAYS his wife Elisabeth conceived." "AFTER THOSE DAYS"* means that Elisabeth conceived right after the 15 days of Zacharias' ministry in the temple when he immediately came home to her. Now, according to our chart, there would be nine days left in July when Zacharias came home to Elisabeth. It appears from our text that Elisabeth conceived on the first of those nine days, but surely all would agree that it was within those last nine days of July.

Such being the case the computing of the time (the month) of Jesus' birth is a simple matter from here on. Luke 1:57 tells us that John was not a premature baby. His mother carried him a full nine months. Luke 1:26 and 36 tell us that Elisabeth conceived six months before Mary, which would make John six months older than Jesus. Luke 2:6 shows us that Jesus was a nine month baby and was not premature.

Now, consulting the chart, we see that when Mary conceived of the Holy Spirit, Elisabeth had conceived six months earlier and Jesus was born nine months later. It is now just a matter of simple addition. Six months plus nine months equals 15 months from the time Elisabeth conceived until Jesus was born. Counting 15 months from July of one year, would bring you to October of the following year the time of Jesus' birth. Simply stated, then, Elisabeth conceived in July and Mary conceived the following January. Thus, as our chart shows, John was born in April and Jesus was born in October.

I am indebted to Rev. Ralph I. Yarnell, D.D. of Marietta, Ohio for the Bible research that produced the foregoing information. It was taken with his permission from the booklet "Should Christians Observe Christmas?" which he published in 1958.

When The Christmas Story (An Introduction) was published in WEEC's Radio Guide, before the publication of the first edition, the responses received were quite interesting and varied so far as this matter of Jesus' birthday being celebrated on December 25th was concerned. We know this date was taken from pagan ceremonies that were practiced long before Christ was born. It is also true that in no place in the Bible are we instructed to observe His birthday in any way, and particularly not as we see it celebrated today. Since we still don't know on what day of the month He was born, or exactly what year for that matter, we couldn't observe His actual birthday if we wanted to. Nor, are we instructed in the Bible to observe Good Friday, Easter, Thanksgiving or any other of the many so-called "religious holidays" that are common to most of us. Yet, for some reason we don't seem to get as excited about the scriptural error involved in celebrating these days. We can always seem to rationalize to suit our needs.

But the world being what it is, and for whatever rationale they want to use for doing it, it has decided to celebrate Christmas on December 25th, as Jesus' birthday. And for the most part this is the only time some people ever give Jesus a moment's thought, if they think of Him at all.

Such being the case, it has always seemed to me that in these "religious holidays" the world is opening up to you and me, as believers in the Lord Jesus Christ, regular opportunities throughout each year to speak a word of witness for Christ, when, as you might say, the world sees it as natural that we should do so.

There are no bona fide "religious holidays" for the Christian at any time throughout the year. The nearest thing we have to such a holiday is the Lord's Day, and that comes around every Sunday. But the world has provided us with bona fide opportunities for witness on their holidays, and we ought to make the most of them.

Paul demonstrated this attitude in Acts 17:22-34 when he used the many statues to the UNKNOWN GOD in Athens, as the means of bringing his witness for the only TRUE GOD, to these Athenians as he spoke from Mars Hill.

Paul's instructions to the believers at Rome about the observance of special days (Rom. 14:5-9) should be of some help to us in this matter also. *Why* we do what we do is far more important than *what* we do, or the *day* on which we do it. If observing any day is a means of edifying yourself and other believers, and making Christ more real and personal to you, then by all means observe that day as unto the Lord, and as a means of witness for Him. But if you can't use it as an occasion for witness for Christ it is questionable whether such an observance is honoring to God at all.

One person wrote to me and provided several items of useful information relative to the practices and customs surrounding Christmas, and backed them all up with good information sources. The letter was concluded with the question, "Now, should we celebrate Christmas or observe 'God's Holy Days' given in the book of Leviticus chapter 23?"

This was a particularly interesting question to me at that time because I was doing an in depth study of the book of Hebrews, wherein the writer of Hebrews was showing to the Jews in Jerusalem in 67 AD the fact that all the Old Testament laws, ordinances and practices including the holidays, had as their sole purpose the foreshadowing of the coming Messiah (Christ). But once Christ had come in the flesh, all of these Old Testament laws, ordinances, practices and holy days were rendered useless. You don't fool around with shadows when the real thing is come.

So to answer this person's question, and maybe others have had the same question, if you do not feel that you should celebrate Christmas as the world does, or even as other Christians do, don't do it. We have no command to do so. But we do have in Hebrews as a theme going throughout the book specific instructions showing us that the Mosaic Law with all its trappings, and even its priesthood were to be done away with and superseded by a better covenant. But any occasion, celebrated or just experienced that will drive you deeper into the Word, in order that you may know more fully the mind of Christ (I Cor. 2:16), is an occasion to rejoice and celebrate. Such was my experience with The Real Christmas Story and it is my prayer that it may be a source of blessing and challenge to you.

12th Month ADAR	1st Month ABIB	2nd Month ZIF	3rd Month SISAN	4th Month THAMMUZ	5th Month AB	6th Month ELUL
24.	1. 2. 3.	4.	5. 6. 7.	8. 9.	10. 11.	12.
Maaziah	Jehoiarib, Jedaiah, Hirim	Seorim	Malchijah, Mijamin, Hakkoz	Abijah or Abia, Jeshuah	Sheaniah, Eliashib	Jakim
MARCH	APRIL	MAY	JUNE	JULY	AUG.	SEPT.
				9 days / 15 days		
3rd Month	4th Month	5th Month	6th Month	7th Month	8th Month	9th Month
			Elizabeth Conceived		John Born	Jesus Born
					Mary Conceived	

Elizabeth   6 Months
Mary   9 Months
Total   15 Months

From the conception of
John the Baptist to the
Birth of Jesus is 15 Months

July

1. Aug.
2. Sept.
3. Oct.
4. Nov.
5. Dec.
6. January
7. Feb.
8. March
9. April
10. May
11. June
12. July
13. Aug.
14. Sept.
15. October

Chart prepared by Rev. Ralph I. Yarnell, D. D. - Marietta, Ohio
(Used by Permission)